D1594417

The Priority of Prudence

THE PRIORITY OF PRUDENCE
Virtue and Natural Law in Thomas Aquinas
and the Implications for Modern Ethics

Daniel Mark Nelson

The Pennsylvania State University Press
University Park, Pennsylvania

Library of Congress Cataloging-in-Publication Data

Nelson, Daniel Mark.
    The priority of prudence : virtue and natural law in Thomas
Aquinas and the implications for modern ethics / Daniel Mark Nelson.
        p.   cm.
    Includes bibliographical references and index.
    ISBN 0-271-00778-8 (alk. paper)
    1. Prudence—History of doctrines—Middle Ages, 600–1500.
    2. Prudence. 3. Thomas, Aquinas, Saint, 1225?–1274—Ethics.
    4. Thomas, Aquinas, Saint, 1225?–1274—Contributions in doctrine of
prudence. 5. Christian ethics—Catholic authors. 6. Virtues.
    7. Natural law. I. Title.
    BV4647.P8N45 1991
    241′.4—dc20   91-6776
                                                                                      CIP

It is the policy of The Pennsylvania State University Press to use acid-free paper for the
first printing of all clothbound books. Publications on uncoated stock satisfy the
minimum requirements of American National Standard for Information Sciences—
Permanence of Paper for Printed Library Materials, ANSI Z39.48–1984.

*For John Foster Nelson
and Alice Heller Nelson*

CONTENTS

PREFACE

Prudence, traditionally characterized as a cardinal virtue, has been maligned and misunderstood in the modern world. For the most part, prudence tends to be seen as a virtue to which careful insurance underwriters should aspire, a trait no one should cultivate to excess. It has connotations, in recent times, of undue caution and selfish calculation. In fact, prudence is sometimes portrayed as a vice. Some of this modern suspicion might be traceable to early reactions against Niccolò Machiavelli's *The Prince*, where the choice between conventional political morality and a new version of prudent politics is dramatized. Machiavelli praises prudence, but a prudence divorced from Christian morality and wedded to power. By Immanuel Kant's time, the conflict between morality and prudence is explicit. According to Kant, prudence perverts moral reason. Prudence somehow got a bad name. It not only ceased to be synonymous with morality, it also came to be understood as opposed to morality.

The contrast to the traditional view is startling. For centuries, and within dominant strands of Western culture, the virtue of prudence, properly understood, and the general sphere of ethics and politics were inseparable. For the classical perspective, which has roots in Aristotle as well as the early Church fathers and which continues through Thomas Aquinas, perhaps its most cogent exponent, prudence is nothing less than the virtue that perfects reasoning about human action.

I wish to reclaim the classical conception of prudence. In attempting to do so, I am joining a current discussion initiated by some provocative critics of contemporary moral and political philosophy to revive and rehabilitate the moral tradition of the virtues. For good examples of this endeavor, see Alasdair MacIntyre's *After Virtue* (1981); Stanley Hauerwas's *Vision and Virtue* (1974), *Character and the Christian Life* (1975), and *A Community of Character* (1981); and William Sullivan's *Reconstructing Public Philosophy* (1982). This tradition has various strands, some of which may be in tension with each other, but what most advocates of a return-to-virtue theory are proposing is some variation on the classical theme of the four cardinal virtues—prudence, temperance, fortitude, and justice—found especially in Aristotle and St. Thomas Aquinas. The most frequently cited classical sources are Aristotle's *Nicomachean Ethics* and *Politics* and St. Thomas's *Summa Theologiae, Commentary on the Nicomachean Ethics, De virtutibus cardinalibus,* and *De virtutibus in communi.*

The reconsideration of the classical understanding of the virtues is largely an attempt to disentangle contemporary thinking about ethics and politics from what MacIntyre calls our "modern moral dilemma." He and others have argued that modern moral philosophy leaves us without the ability to resolve moral disagreement. In MacIntyre's account, a series of moral theories emerged in response to the fragmentation and collapse of religious authority. According to his critique, the basic types of competing moral theory successfully refute each other. In the absence of a shared vocabulary for giving one another reasons for adopting or rejecting moral judgments, we find our attempts at moral discourse reduced to assertion or manipulation (1981).

One need not agree with all of the specific claims in MacIntyre's condensed history of ethics in order to acknowledge the force of his analysis of characteristic problems and confusions in modern moral philosophy. Neither does one need to accept his entire critique of modern ethics in order to see the value of reexamining the traditional moral vocabulary. MacIntyre's narrative offers a suggestive description of what happened to the virtues and why they were abandoned so precipitously. His account makes it possible to see how prudence might have received its bad name as a result of some of the historical forces that prompted the rejection of the tradition in which the virtues were embedded. Still, the details and usefulness of the traditional vocabulary of the virtues, and the attributes of individual virtues in particular, need more careful attention.

This study, which deals specifically with the virtue of prudence, is prompted by a conviction that the inadequacy of much contemporary thinking about morality makes a conversation about an ethics of virtue well worth pursuing. It certainly is not *just* the inadequacy of the modern alternatives that makes the virtues interesting; it is also possible that the vocabulary of the virtues provides an especially useful way of dealing with specific moral problems and that its emphasis on the relation between character and community productively challenges our contemporary moral situation. This study's focus on prudence is an attempt to increase the usefulness, interest, and rigor of the reconsideration of the virtues. The main vehicle for this will be an analysis of the extensive and nuanced portrayal of the virtue of prudence by Thomas Aquinas.

This appropriation of Thomas's discussion of the virtues must be made in the face of a puzzling difficulty: According to the standard readings Thomas is not a theorist of prudence, or even of virtue in general, but of natural law. If the common natural-law interpretations of Thomas attend to the virtue of prudence at all, they tend to assign prudence the role of merely specifying what specific actions come under the natural law and the task of implementing its dictates. On the other hand, although a few commentators do call attention to the importance of prudence (Josef Pieper, 1965, is a good example), explicating Thomas's ethics by emphasizing the significance and interaction of the cardinal virtues, little is said to reconcile Thomas's teaching about virtue with his discussion of natural law. From either perspective, the relation between natural law and prudence remains unexplained or inadequately understood. According to a theory of natural law, moral rules are deduced from naturally known universal principles. According to an ethics of prudence, right reason about human acts depends on experience and habituation to the virtues. The two themes do not easily coexist as accounts of morality, but the tension between these themes in the interpretation of Thomas is not widely recognized or resolved.

In short, there is an important problem in the interpretation of Thomas's ethics. The significance that he seems to attribute to prudence does not fit well with the standard natural-law reading. If his ethics is in fact essentially a natural-law ethics, then prudence is merely the virtue that determines means to naturally known ends. But if prudence, according to Thomas, is more than right reason about means for achieving the good, if knowledge about right ends also depends on prudence working in harmony with the other cardinal virtues, then there is a tension between the claims for prudence and the interpretations that stress natural law.

I argue for an interpretation that resolves the difficulty by showing how Thomas's understanding of ethics is more thoroughly prudential than generally assumed. In other words, my thesis is that for Thomas, the moral life as well as reflection on it depend on prudence and not on knowledge of the natural law—at least not the versions of natural law commonly attributed to him. The interpretive challenge that I face is to explain the texts usually read as giving priority to the ability of the habit of *synderesis* (a kind of moral instinct) to know the content of the natural law and as limiting prudence to the service of naturally known first principles.

This study, in summary, is conceived as a contribution to the contemporary debate about virtue as well as to the long and variegated discussion of Thomas Aquinas's ethics. The two objects are closely related: The focus on Thomas is the means for entering the current conversation responsibly and, I hope, productively. Recent talk about the virtues did not come from nowhere; it is part of a longstanding moral tradition. Thomas refined a moral vocabulary he inherited and worked out its application to his own situation. Modern theorists attempting to reclaim the virtues for contemporary cultivation are likely to need a rehabilitated understanding of prudence. St. Thomas is an entirely appropriate place to begin.

Within the context of Thomistic ethics, a prudential ethics, properly understood, provides an attractive alternative to the ahistorical rigidity of the common articulation of natural law and to the equally problematic existential and situational theories that have reacted against it. More generally, this interpretation of Thomas Aquinas has the potential of illuminating the way out of parallel predicaments characteristic of contemporary moral philosophy. For example, a rehabilitated ethics of virtue centered on prudence might constitute a workable alternative to both Kantianism and consequentialism.

Chapter 1 presents a brief overview of the natural-law tradition in order to show how Thomas is ordinarily located at its very center. For many commentators, classical natural-law thinking culminates in Thomas, whose teaching is seen as the tradition's standard of orthodoxy. In addition, the chapter contains a summary of the way Thomas's discussion of natural law is most often understood. According to the common view, natural law is located in a hierarchy of law that stretches from the most particular specifications of the positive law in local communities to God's law for the universe. On this account, humans have the innate ability to know the more or less general principles of morality contained within the law of nature and to deduce from them conclusions about right and wrong in particular circumstances.

Chapters 2 and 3 contain a detailed explication of Thomas's understanding of prudence, beginning with the context in which he situated his discussion of the virtues: the circumstances of human acts, the will's orientation to the good, and the passions. Chapter 3 provides enough information about how Thomas understood the components of prudence and the spheres in which it operates to make it a usable concept for contemporary discussion and a desirable virtue for cultivation. Much of the task of describing Thomas's portrayal of prudence has already been accomplished in other studies, but the discussion here is distinguished by its orientation to two central questions: How can what Thomas says about prudence be reconciled with what he says about natural law? And what are the implications of prudence for contemporary ethics?

The most direct challenge to prevailing interpretations of Thomas occurs in Chapter 4. In very brief summary, I argue that for Thomas there is indeed such a thing as a doctrine of natural law, but it serves to explain rather than to guide practical reasoning. Except in its most vague and general principle—do good and avoid evil—and except as a way of speaking about the observed patterns of inclinations of God's creation to various ends, the content of natural law, which is primarily a matter of God's will and knowledge, is unavailable to independent human reason. Our knowledge of what specific ends to pursue and of the appropriate means to employ depends on prudence and the other cardinal virtues governing right reason and desire.

In this chapter I substantiate a reading of the natural-law passages in Thomas that is compatible with his discussion of prudence and virtue and that saves him from the later deductive and legalistic natural-law tradition. The two main themes in Chapter 4 are that his analysis of the moral life has much more to do with prudence than natural law and that practical reasoning is nourished by experience and habituation rather than by independent knowledge of divine or natural law.

The fifth and last chapter is related to but not ultimately dependent on the preceding discussion of Thomas. That is, I believe Thomas provides a compelling and coherent account of the moral life in terms of the four cardinal virtues, which in turn depend on the activity of prudence. This is not a claim about Thomas the "Universal Teacher" of a "Perennial

Philosophy," however, and it is by no means an argument from authority. Even if it turned out that conflicting interpretations of Thomas were more persuasive than the one proposed here, the question would still remain whether something like the understanding of ethics that is oriented to prudence and virtue has contemporary relevance. I believe it does: It provides a vocabulary for dealing with concrete cases and individual agents that is arguably more useful than the alternatives. At a more reflective level, this way of talking about ethics inclines moral philosophy against the tendency to claim ahistorical and universal status for moral intuitions and judgments while also resisting relativism and consequentialism. A prudential ethics has the added advantage of having something to say in the contemporary debate while still being able to situate itself in a particular tradition. I hope this investigation into the virtue of prudence assists in the development of a theory of virtue that will prove an important alternative to the present state of moral philosophy. Even though my project is intended as a contribution to attempts at reviving the virtues, I also see it as a challenge to those attempts. According to St. Thomas, although the cardinal virtues depend on each other, prudence is especially important: It "in-forms" the other virtues. Most recent discussion about virtue has little to say about prudence and how it might be cultivated and sustained in our culture. If Thomas is correct, if something like his account of prudence is taken seriously, one cannot adequately talk about or promote virtue without attending to prudence. Attempts to recover a context for the virtues thus require a recovery of prudence, but an understanding of prudence and what it entails suggests the difficulty of the task.

ACKNOWLEDGMENTS

I owe debts of gratitude to my parents, my wife, fellow students, and to my teachers and colleagues for whatever merits this study in the ethics of St. Thomas Aquinas possesses.

Without the benefit of parents whose lives demonstrate the theological and moral virtues, I never would have begun the study of religion and ethics. Without support from my wife and best friend Deborah, I never would have been able to continue that endeavor. Without the camaraderie of my fellow students in the Department of Religion at Princeton University, the time in which this project was begun would have been a much less happy and fruitful period in my life. And without the example and training of exceptional teachers, deficiencies in my education and in this project would be much more substantial and apparent.

I owe specific thanks to four teachers in particular. I came to Princeton's Department of Religion to work with Professor Paul Ramsey, who died in 1988. He constantly challenged my thinking, broadened my understanding, and inspired me through his example of scholarship, teaching, engagement in public affairs, and Christian commitment. Professor Ramsey was an extraordinarily generous friend and mentor. I have also been fortunate in receiving the benefit of the complementary virtues of my two main academic advisors, Professors Jeffrey Stout and Victor Preller. To Professor Preller, whose knowledge of Thomas Aquinas is as incisive as it is encyclopedic, I owe not only much of the idea for the main thesis in this study but also many felicitous ways of illustrating it. A number of the examples I use are gratefully borrowed directly from him. I also owe him thanks for instruction and guidance in the theological context of Thomas's ethics. Professor Jeffrey Stout was more than I could have hoped for in an advisor. His friendship, provocative teaching, constructive criticism, sensitivity as a reader to nuances of style and content, and unfailing practical wisdom have been especially formative in my academic as well as personal development. Finally, I am grateful to Professor Paul Sigmund, of Princeton's Politics Department, for instruction in the history of natural-law thinking and for his careful reading of this study. Professor Sigmund, whose interpretation of Thomas's ethics differs from the one presented here, generously played the helpful role of friendly critic.

I also owe thanks to several sources of support during the period in which I was working on this book: The Charlotte W. Newcombe Foundation provided a very generous fellowship to support a year's research and writing. Princeton University provided opportunities for me to teach and to work on the staffs of Mathey College and of the University Chapel. The Dean of the College Office at Dartmouth College provided time and assistance, which allowed me to bring the manuscript to a publishable form.

Thanks to the assistance of these people and unnamed others, I have come to appreciate the truth of Thomas's insight that "in order to do well, whether in the works of the active life or in the activity of the contemplative life, man needs the help of friends" (*S.T.* I-II, q. 4, a. 8).

A note on citations: There are no footnotes in the following pages, but passages and persons cited are identified in the text. Full bibliographic information appears in the final section, "Sources." My main source for this study is St. Thomas Aquinas's *Summa Theologiae*, abbreviated as *S.T.* As illustrated above, I follow the standard shorthand for specifying the main division of the *Summa* (in this case usually I-II or II-II), the question (q.), and the article (a.) from which a quotation is taken or to which a reference is made.

1

THE NATURAL LAWYERS' INTERPRETATION OF THOMAS AQUINAS

Sometimes in the history of philosophy the defense of a particular philosophical position and the interpretation of a particular philosopher become closely identified.
— Alasdair MacIntyre

His moral philosophy is of particular interest. It is dominated by the concept of natural law, and what Aquinas has to say on the subject is related, on the one hand, to practical questions, such as sexual conduct, about which moralists argue, and, on the other hand, to logical questions, such as whether or not judgments of moral value can be deduced from statements of empirical fact, about which lively discussion goes on among moral philosophers.
— W. D. Hudson

I

W. D. Hudson is not a natural-law theorist, but his perception of Thomas Aquinas's moral philosophy as an ethics of natural law is almost universally shared, the product of centuries of interpretation informed by theories of natural law. Most philosophers, theologians, and historians of moral and political thought, whether Thomists or not, assume that a rich doctrine of natural law forms the foundation for Thomas's thinking about ethics and politics. That perception, I shall argue, is mistaken. A careful reading of the relevant texts suggests that the Aristotelian vocabulary of the virtues, and especially the cardinal virtue of prudence, controls most of what Thomas says about morality. This vocabulary, to be sure, is theologically tamed. Aristotle's standard of moral measurement, the virtuous individual living in a good society, is only the penultimate word in Thomistic ethics because ultimately the common good and end of humanity is found in God, not the polis. A theology of grace, for Thomas, is a necessary supplement to a morality of virtue. Nonetheless, Thomas still finds it possible to speak of the natural good for humans, apart from their supernatural end.

According to the standard interpretation, natural law comprises the central premises of Thomas's teaching about natural morality. The virtues, if they are treated at all, carry out the task of motivating individuals to act in accordance with law. Prudence is the virtue enabling one to apply the law to particular cases. In contrast, according to the interpretation I shall defend, prudence and the virtues are primary. One looks to the accumulated moral wisdom and the habitual behavior and judgments of virtuous individuals in one's community as the basic source of information about the rightness and wrongness of human action. Natural law functions theologically to explain how the world, created by a rational and purposive God, contains as much agreement about virtue as it does, but natural law is not a source of moral information specific enough to be immediately useful for guiding conduct.

This study begins with the supposition that the standard emphasis on natural law has been read into Thomas by his disciples and admirers and accepted at face value by his modern critics. Although one way of establishing this claim would be to trace the introduction and development of particular natural-law themes in the history of Thomistic interpretation, I choose to begin by defending an alternative reading of Thomas Aquinas that stresses the central importance of virtue.

A summary description of the conventional natural-law interpretation of Thomas Aquinas will serve as a prologue to the alternative reading that stresses virtue. The task of relating the established interpretation has its own set of difficulties. Because I charge that we have inherited a misreading of Aquinas, I would particularly like to avoid misrepresenting his commentators. The following sketch of the standard interpretations of Thomistic ethics, derived from more extensive portraits by others, is intended to be only detailed enough to illustrate fairly the main features shared by the standard explications. At the same time, my treatment aims to retain enough generality to allow room for the variety evident in the vast amount of relevant scholarship. For my purposes, a focus on the broad agreement underlying the interpretation of St. Thomas is instructive. For other purposes it would be important to stress the fact that neither now nor in St. Thomas's own time has natural law constituted a single doctrine or theory in all its details. Thomas had several variations on the theme of natural law with which to work, and subsequent commentators have been the recipients and vehicles of many more.

A. P. d'Entreves begins his classic history and analysis of natural-law thinking by noting the diversity of meanings associated with the very notion of natural law, which "was laden with ambiguity even in the days when it was considered self-evident" (d'Entreves 1951: 7). He argues, for example, that medieval and modern natural-law theories share little besides the name, that there are many traditions of natural law rather than one, and that variations in the meaning of the reference to nature have had profoundly different practical implications (1951: 8–15). Does the law of nature refer to the entire natural order or to human nature in particular? If it refers to human nature, is human reason itself, human nature in its entirety, or the nature of human society the source of moral information? Questions like these could be and have been multiplied by defenders and critics of natural law alike.

Granting the important observation that oversimplifying natural-law thinking sacrifices accuracy for the sake of clarity, it is still possible to make some responsible generalizations. Paul Sigmund's description of the basic features of the extended family of natural-law theories adequately identifies the basic kind of moral and political thinking commonly discerned in Thomas Aquinas and characteristic of the broad intellectual tradition in which he is ordinarily situated: The "central assertion expressed or implied in most theories of natural law . . . is the belief that there exists in nature and/or in human nature a rational order which can provide intelligible value-statements independently of human will, that are universal in application, unchangeable in their ultimate content, and morally obligatory on mankind" (Sigmund 1971: viii).

This very general notion, in all its diverse and sometimes conflicting articulations, has a history with roots in the pre-Socratic philosophers, with vigorous branches in medieval Europe, and even a few offshoots in contemporary philosophy, although most versions of natural law were rejected in favor of alternatives two centuries ago. According to the standard account, Thomas Aquinas provides an especially coherent articulation of natural-law thinking. His teaching is commonly regarded as a successful synthesis of the versions of natural law he inherited and as the foundation for subsequent variations. For the critics of natural law, the version attributed to Thomas is the version to refute. Before considering the content of the Thomistic theory of natural law, however, I shall briefly review how Thomas is ordinarily situated at the very center of the natural-law tradition. My sketch of that tradition, and of Thomas's customary place within it, is a distillation of the standard account, a short synopsis of the narrative that the natural lawyers tell about themselves. Although my overall discussion of Thomas's ethics might contribute to part of a revised history of the natural-law tradition, these next few pages of summary are not presented as revisionist history themselves, but rather as the outlines of a very familiar history told in detail often enough by others.

II

The story proper, told in roughly the same way by the standard textbooks and histories, begins with a kind of family history, an attempt to trace the lineage of natural law back as far as possible to the origins of Greek philosophy. (See Sigmund, 1971, for a brief rendition of the standard narrative, representative quotations from the important texts, and a useful bibliography.) The line of descent, at least in the version of the story that wants to document a rather extended family, seems to begin with Pythagoras and his followers and their speculations about numerical principles simultaneously governing the material world and guiding human conduct. The general notion of moral principles inherent in nature was subsequently appropriated by the Sophists in Athens and employed in critiques of existing laws and institutions. Socrates is an important figure in the genealogy because of his professed obedience to a standard transcending conventional norms and because of his apparent conviction that the achievement of excellence and virtue depend on knowledge of the true natures of things. In Plato's *Republic*, the connection between principles located in nature and claims about the moral order is more explicit. His version of a just society is based on his vision of an harmonious and hierarchical ordering, universal in human nature, according to which the principle of desire is subordinated to the principle of spirit and spirit is subordinated to reason. For society, that means that the few individuals most endued with reason ought to rule.

None of these figures is associated with a full-fledged theory of natural law, which does not appear until after Aristotle. His ethics are ordinarily read as an ethics of virtue in which the virtue of *phronesis,* or prudence, determines the "golden mean" of behavior in particular situations, although the epistemic value of the concept of the mean is a matter of dispute. When Thomas Aquinas is read as a natural-law theorist by many of his critics, his appropriation of Aristotle is often seen as a distortion of genuine Aristotelianism for natural-law purposes. Other readers of Aristotle, however, discern in the *Politics* and especially in the *Nicomachean Ethics* the foundations of an admittedly undeveloped natural-law doctrine entirely compatible with the standard account of Thomistic ethics. (See Harry V. Jaffa, 1952, for a discussion of this issue.)

Natural law emerges for the first time as an explicit philosophical theory with the Stoics and with the Roman emperor Justinian. The Stoic themes are summarized by Cicero in *The Commonwealth* and *The Laws:* Natural law is congruent with the reason by which the universe is governed, knowable by human reason, and amenable to emulation in the conduct of human affairs. It forms the foundation for all positive law, binds individual human communities into a universal human society, and includes sanctions for transgression. Unchanging and eternal, it applies to everyone at all times and in all places.

This grand vision was received and elaborated in diverse ways by the Roman lawyers and incorporated, along with material from the Roman jurists Ulpian, Paulus, and Gaius, in Justinian's monumental codification of law, the *Corporis iuris civilis,* compiled in the first part of the sixth century. The code includes a great diversity of material, some of it providing conflicting accounts of the organization and content of natural law (*ius naturale*) and its relation to the civil law of states (*ius civile*) and the common law of nations (*ius gentium*). According to d'Entreves, the special importance of Justinian's collection for the natural-law tradition is its magnification of the dignity of law. Part of the grandeur of the compilation, derived in large part from its foundation in natural law, is its universality and its appeal to reason rather than to force (d'Entreves 1951: 17–32).

The religious conversion of natural law moves the story toward its climax, as the standard account would have it, when the Greek, Stoic, imperial Roman, and Christian themes culminate in the teaching of St. Thomas. A summary of d'Entreves's account of the relevant history illustrates the significance of the heroic role in which Thomas is usually cast: The specifically Christian versions of natural law, drawing on the inheritance of Judaism's divine law, underwent considerable development between the age of the Church fathers and Gratian's twelfth-century collection of canon law. The Stoic and Roman understanding of the law of nature, adopted by the Church fathers, was Christianized by attributing its origin to the God of the Old Testament, who imparted its content to Adam. The Apostle Paul's observation in Romans 2 about the law written in the hearts and consciences of the gentiles gave the doctrine explicit scriptural warrant.

St. Ambrose and St. Augustine both accepted the ability of natural reason to discern good from evil, at least within certain limits, and agreed to some congruence between the moral law naturally known and the law revealed in scripture. But despite this acknowledgment of natural law, the early Christian view remained essentially pessimistic, stressing the distance between nature and grace, reason and revelation, and between the earthly and heavenly kingdoms. This series of conflicts presented a great problem for the development and legitimation of Western culture. In the medieval period the conflicts were resolved, largely via the development of natural-law thinking, and medieval Christianity was able to carry out the task of grounding social and political institutions in reason, giving them a positive value. This task, of course, was most successfully accomplished by Thomas Aquinas through his refinement and synthesis of the preceding natural-law tradition:

> An immense task lay ahead of the medieval man. . . . How could a Christian community be taught the elementary duties of a good life and fellowship? How could the teaching of Aristotle, the pagan philosopher, be adapted to the Christian view of life? If so great a body of wisdom had been discovered without supernatural help, if a basis was to be provided for human relationships independently of the higher requirements of Christian perfection, surely there must be a knowledge of ethical values which man can attain with the sole help of his reason. There must be a system of natural ethics. Its cornerstone must be the natural law.
>
> This entirely new function for the idea of the law of nature is nowhere more apparent than in the teaching of St. Thomas Aquinas. He is the greatest representative of medieval philosophy as well as the most constructive and systematic thinker of the Middle Ages. . . . We can therefore safely choose St. Thomas's theory of natural law as the best illustration of the part which that notion was called upon to play in one of the great constructive periods of Western civilization. (D'Entreves 1951: 38–39)

For d'Entreves, the significance of Thomas's accomplishment goes beyond the synthesis of the preexisting strains of the natural-law tradition. Thomas is situated at the dramatic center of the narrative because he articulated a new and particularly productive version of the relationship between natural reason and revelation: "In giving a clear formulation of this idea, St. Thomas was fulfilling, as it were, what had been the deepest and most intimate aspiration of Medieval Christianity. His assertion that 'Grace does not abolish Nature but perfects it' . . . is the crown of that 'Christian Humanism' which is the essence of his philosophy" (1951: 42). Thomas's description of a human nature potentially perfected by grace and not completely subservient to sin allowed for the successful articulation of a natural and rational morality, d'Entreves says, as well as a rational defense of the moral law and human institutions previously described as "dikes" against sin (ibid.). On this kind of reading, Thomistic natural law is the culmination of the ancient and medieval traditions as well as the origin of much modern moral and political thought, despite the modern era's rejection of Thomas's theology and its emphasis on individual rights.

The narrative becomes more fragmented after Thomas as competing versions of the story draw different lines between its medieval and modern episodes. Sigmund's way of drawing the line is to classify as modern those versions of natural law that tend to be rationalist rather than theologically oriented, individualist rather than communitarian, and politically radical rather than conservative of established institutions and patterns of social relation (Sigmund 1971: 55-56). Another approach is to make Thomas the standard of orthodoxy and to describe subsequent versions of natural law as modern to the extent that they depart from the received reading of Thomas.

Whether they are classified as medieval, transitional, or modern, the next important characters to appear are William of Ockham (1290-1349), Francisco Suárez (1548-1617), and Hugo Grotius (1583-1645). There are also questions about the modernity of Richard Hooker's *Laws of Ecclesiastical Polity*, which appeared in 1593. When the narrative reaches the second half of the seventeenth century, however, the debate between versions shifts from how modern a particular character is to whether or not he even belongs to the original story. Samuel Pufendorf's 1672 treatise *On the Law of Nature and Nations* is obviously within the received tradition, but Thomas Hobbes's *Leviathan* (1651) and John Locke's *Second Treatise of Civil Government* (1689), despite their references to the "state of nature" and occasional employment of natural-law vocabulary, are arguably outside it, or at best at its fringes. Finally, different versions of the story about the rise and fall of natural law end differently, some concluding with Rousseau and others extending the epilogue as far as Kant or even Hegel.

Admittedly, to talk about the end of the natural-law tradition is somewhat misleading. There still are natural-lawyers, and books about natural law are still being written. But even though natural law continues to figure in legal theory, at least until recently, and even though it continues to influence Catholic ethics, although in a diminished way, its force as a coherent and identifiable moral and political doctrine has long been spent. Its claim as a compelling philosophical theory is understood, at least by most professional philosophers, to have been refuted. Whether the final chapter is written in a tragic mode or not, most versions of the story conclude by laying natural law to rest. As a result, Thomas Aquinas, the main character in the story, appears to have only historic interest. If, however, there is a different story that can be told about St. Thomas, a story that makes his usual appearance in the natural-law narrative a case of long-mistaken identity with profound cultural consequences, then there may be reasons to include him in another story—that of the virtues—which deserves contemporary interest.

III

Before examining the identity of the relatively unfamiliar Thomas Aquinas who figures in the story about the tradition of the virtues, a closer review of part of the natural-law narrative may be useful. One of the reasons for recounting that story once again was to emphasize Thomas's prominence in the natural-law tradition. I do not deny that there is *a* Thomas Aquinas who dominates that tradition, but I have reasons for reassessing the standard portrayal of Thomas. Neither do I deny that Thomas has quite a bit to say about natural law. Instead, I challenge the conventional interpretation of his discussion of natural law and question its epistemic importance relative to his discussion of the virtues, especially the virtue of prudence. The present task, however, is to return to the center of the standard narrative in order to see in more detail what it says about the general theory of natural law itself and about the articulation of that theory by the main character, St. Thomas.

First, a caveat: Although there is broad agreement that Thomas teaches a doctrine of natural law, no single interpretation of Thomas exactly approximates the standard account to which I have been referring. The standard account is a kind of ideal type, useful for my purposes because it emphasizes what most interpretations share and allows me to distinguish the way in which my alternative interpretation differs.

The standard account contains certain assumptions about Thomas's ethics—particularly that it is an ethics of natural law—and assumes a set of philosophical problems that have to be solved in order to establish or defend the validity of the doctrine. Within that general framework, there is room for considerable disagreement about the extent to which the solutions to those problems can be found in Thomas's teaching. There is also room for debate about what constitutes a viable solution and for discussion about how to interpret what might be Thomas's solutions. Some marginal interpretations, on the fringes of the standard account, tend to accept its general assumptions. An analysis of the philosophical problems and of the Thomistic texts, however, leads some readers to supplement Thomas's theory with a "necessary complement" (Karl Rahner) or to challenge the established characterization of Thomas's theory of natural law itself (John Finnis). Such distinctions should be kept in mind during the course of the following review.

The interpreters I cite by way of example were not selected because they articulate readings with which every other interpreter would agree in all respects, but because most interpreters would agree in the most telling respects. They were chosen because they articulate some of the common assumptions (Thomas J. Higgins) or because in their discussion of some of the problems encountered by Thomistic natural law, they closely approximate the standard account (R. A. Armstrong). This is not to deny that various other readings of Thomas might differ from the reading reviewed here, because at some detailed levels of analysis and for some interpretive purposes the differences are admittedly significant. For purposes of this analysis, however, the important point is how much the standard readings of Thomas have in common.

One modern rendition of Thomistic natural law begins by defining ethics as "the philosophical science," distinguished from sociology and history, that establishes the rightness of human action "in light of first principles" and "universal, immutable moral laws which are as valid as the laws of chemistry and physics." It is metaphysically grounded and thus rooted "in the bedrock of reality" (Higgins 1958: 6,9). The kind of obligation with which this science is concerned "arises only from the reason and will of a superior embodied in law": the eternal law, which is God's ordering of the universe, and the natural law, which is God's direction of his creatures via intrinsic principles (1958: 85). The natural law, which mirrors, although darkly, God's eternal law in human reason, is "man's awareness that certain conduct is necessarily good, certain other necessarily evil" (1958: 89). Its judgments are formulated in principles, analogous in certainty to the principles of logic, mathematics, and the physical sciences, which are directly derived from human nature. God has created human reason with the ability to apprehend and formulate the general principles of the law of nature, but further specifications are evident only to those with "training and experience" (1958: 91-92).

Higgins identifies Thomas's first principle of natural law as "do good and avoid evil." When this principle is applied to "the essential needs and situations of human life," he notes, a number of secondary principles immediately and easily can be inferred from it, for example: Parents ought to care for their children. Children ought to honor their parents. Theft is wrong. Murder is wrong. "No man whose reason is developed can in any way be ignorant of the primary principles of Natural Law," Higgins says. "While he cannot be invincibly ignorant of the secondary principles, he may at times be invincibly ignorant of some tertiary principles," which forbid the less immediately evident evils of "polygamy, divorce, dueling, and contraception" (1958: 122). Knowledge of the science of ethics, combined with a good conscience, which is reason's "practical application of speculative truths already possessed" (1958: 131), and aided by the virtue of prudence, which "is the ability to discern the true ends of human conduct and to fashion the means appropriate to those ends," (1958: 152), is sufficient for the whole of natural morality. Parts two and three of Higgins's, book, in which this version of the Thomistic method is employed to determine the principles of individual and social ethics, contain determinations of the natural law regarding specific moral and political topics ranging from the evils of masturbation to the need for an international political authority.

Such a college-textbook portrayal of Thomistic ethics is perhaps less nuanced than other contemporary versions, but most commentators ascribe to Thomas a theory of natural law that bears a strong resemblance to Higgins's explication. They also place St. Thomas at the center of the natural-law tradition. Leo Strauss says that the Christian version of natural law "reached its theoretical perfection in the work of Thomas Aquinas...which is the classic form of natural law teaching" (1968: 82-83). The *New Catholic Encyclopedia* points out that "it remained for St. Thomas to perfect the idea of natural law" (Brown 1967: 251-56). Even for John Finnis, who makes substantial criticisms of conventional interpretations, Thomas is the "paradigm" theorist of natural law, dominating the tradition's history since the beginning of the Christian era, "synthesizing" its various strains, and "fixing the vocabulary and to some extent the doctrine of later scholastic and, therefore, early modern thought" (Finnis 1980: 28). Further examples of this estimation of St. Thomas could be multiplied, although scholars differ over the specifics of his most noteworthy theoretical achievements.

The tradition with which Thomas is so intimately associated is generally described as a philosophical theory of ethics and politics centered on the notion of law. The natural law not only commands right action and prohibits wrong action, it is also the standard for distinguishing right from wrong. Natural law is the timeless, independent, universal, and absolute "higher law," although Christian versions of the theory, at least in their classical forms, place it in the context of God's divine law. Natural law underlies, justifies, and also judges all human law, morality, and institutions. As will become apparent in the following description of standard accounts of the actual operation of natural law—that is, its specific relation to other kinds of law, how it is known, what its content is, and how it can be applied—it is ordinarily presented as a deductive system in which conclusions in the form of specific moral judgments are derived from premises, a hierarchy of fundamental principles grounded in an essential human nature.

IV

Natural law, according to most accounts related to the standard Thomistic versions, is a sphere of law located in a hierarchy that stretches from the immutable principles of God's eternal law for the universe to the most specific ordinances of local civil law. Eternal law is God's reason manifested in his plan for and sustenance of creation. In this context, law has two senses: On the one hand, the eternal law refers to the principles that govern the operation of creation, including but not restricted to the principles about which the physical sciences are concerned. On the other hand, the eternal law refers to God's will and knowledge of required and prohibited conduct, the moral law as it exists in the mind of God.

In the traditional Christian understanding of the theory, natural law is grounded and included in eternal law; it is constituted by that part of God's law for human action discernible by natural human reason through its apprehension of intrinsic principles operative in human nature. The "key statement" of Thomistic moral theory, according to Higgins, is "that the Eternal Law exists and operates in man and as such is called the Natural Law. . . . It is man's awareness that certain conduct is necessarily good, certain other necessarily evil. . . . The mind of man must clearly mirror the eternal law for man" (1958: 89). But because humans were created for a supernatural end, the achievement of which exceeds the abilities of human nature unaided by grace, and because human reason itself is deficient in many ways as a result of sin, even perfect knowledge of the natural law is insufficient. God therefore revealed his will in scripture, making part of the natural law explicit and supplementing it with requirements for salvation. This revelation is called the divine law.

Human law, at the other end of the hierarchy, is subdivided into the *ius gentium*, the "law of nations," and the *ius civile*, a community's positive "civil law," distinctions made originally in Roman law. The *ius gentium* was the broad sphere of law distinguished from the explicitly Roman *ius civile* and was employed in cases where parties to a dispute were not under the jurisdiction of the same legal code. Regarded as a further specification or affirmation of the law of nature, it was the law common to all nations, a product of shared human reason.

Late scholastic and early modern interest in codifying the natural law in the process of developing international law embellished the legalism of this whole hierarchy, perhaps one of the reasons Thomas's ethical and political teaching has so frequently been read by his successors in terms of an overarching legal doctrine. (See Herbert E. Hartmann, Jr., 1979, for a discussion of how an inauthentic legalism has been read into St. Thomas's references to natural law, which Hartmann argues has little to do with any notion of a legal code.) For example, George Sabine, a historian of political thought, states that "the universality of law was a fundamental conception" for St. Thomas, whose task as a political theorist was to explicate the connections between human and divine law, via natural law: "Human law was for him part and parcel of the whole system of divine government whereby everything both in heaven and earth is ruled. Such a system Thomas regarded as quite literally an emanation from the reason of God, regulating the relationships between all creatures.... Law in the narrower human sense was therefore merely one aspect... of a cosmic fact" (Sabine 1937: 247, 251–52). It follows, according to such a view, that the answers to questions about the justification of human legislation and institutions can be found by inquiring into human nature because of the corollary relationship between human law and natural law, "which merely needs to be made definite and effective in order to provide for the exigencies of human life or of special circumstances of human life" (1937: 255).

D. J. O'Connor's discussion of Thomas's teaching on how the natural law is known begins, as do most accounts, by attributing to him a doctrine of intellectually intuitable human essences from which normative principles are derived. That is, the basis of Thomas's moral theory is the notion that human nature can be defined in terms of specific essential attributes (O'Connor 1967: 15). The link between essential human nature and moral obligation is a set of universally shared natural human inclinations. Humans share with all things an inclination to preserve their very being, with all other animals they are inclined to reproduce their species and to raise their young, and as rational creatures humans are inclined to live in society and to know the truth about God. On the basis of these inclinations, we are supposedly able to intuit the general principles of what we ought to do by employing an innate moral "sense" known by the troublesome technical term *synderesis*.

The meaning of synderesis is intertwined with the notion of conscience. Eric D'Arcy's study of the Christian concept of conscience describes how the Church inherited from Greek and Roman philosophy the notion of a "judicial conscience" that judges past action, and how from St. Paul it obtained the notion of a "legislative conscience" that directs the course of future action (D'Arcy 1961: 3–15). According to D'Arcy, a passage in St. Jerome's commentary on Ezekiel "confused the whole matter with a new term and a new metaphor," which profoundly influenced and complicated the subsequent discussion of conscience. According to Jerome's comments on Ezekiel 1:5–14, the prophet's vision of an eagle signifies something called synderesis, a Latinized Greek term of disputed origin (perhaps the result of a copyist's error), which Jerome describes as a superior kind of conscience (D'Arcy 1961: 16–17). Jerome's description of synderesis, taken up by Peter Lombard, fueled a century's debate about the relation between synderesis and conscience and whether to characterize synderesis as a faculty or a habit. Once firmly entrenched in the vocabulary, it had to be assigned some function. For Thomas in the *Summa,* it generally is concerned with the apprehension of the first principles of natural law (D'Arcy 1961: 18-19).

In order to understand this function of synderesis, it may help to note the distinction Thomas makes between the speculative and practical intellect, a distinction which refers to two distinct operations of the human reason, not two different human intellects. The speculative operation of the intellect is concerned with "being," with understanding things that are already "out there" in the world and not subject to human creation. The practical operation of the intellect is concerned with things humans make and do, the spheres of art and morality. Synderesis is the practical intellect's habit of knowing the first principles of its own activity, the first of which is that good is to be pursued and evil avoided. It is analogous to *intellectus,* the habit of apprehending the first principles of the speculative intellect, such as the "principle of contradiction" stating that nothing can both be and not be at the same time. When the basic human inclinations, which have their foundation in eternal law, are "raised to the intentional order by *synderesis,* " they become "the precepts of the natural law" (Spinnenweber 1972: 12).

There is considerable scholarly disagreement about how Thomas understood the specifics of the process of knowing the natural law. F. C. Copleston, S.J., who argues for a kind of intuition of the natural law, augmented by "reflection and discussion," and who resists interpretations that make knowledge of the law a simple matter of deduction, provides a good middle-of-the-road summary:

> [A]lthough man cannot read off, as it were, the eternal law in God's mind, he can discern the fundamental tendencies and needs of his nature, and by reflecting on them he can come to a knowledge of the natural moral law. Every man possesses the natural inclinations to the development of his potentialities and the attainment of the good for man. Every man possesses also the light of reason whereby he can reflect on these fundamental inclinations of his nature and promulgate to himself the natural moral law, which is the totality of the universal precepts or dictates of right reason concerning the good which is to be pursued and the evil which is to be shunned. By the light of his own

reason, therefore, man can arrive at some knowledge of the natural law. (Copleston 1955: 213)

Thomas's own very general statement, which will be considered in more detail in subsequent chapters, is that all the specific precepts of natural law follow from its very first principle, "that good is to be done and pursued, and evil is to be avoided," and that "the order of the precepts of the natural law follows the order of the natural inclinations" (*S.T.* I–II, 94.2). Sigmund's description of Thomas's natural-law teaching notes that the precepts are "related to" the inclinations but also include additional commandments and prohibitions: "Among the practices which Aquinas condemns as opposed to nature are theft,... adultery, homosexuality, usury,... drunkenness, gluttony, suicide, murder, and the violation of promises. Among the commands of the natural law he includes the care of children by their parents, reverence for God, charity to the poor, and obedience to the law" (Sigmund 1971: 40; who cites *S.T.* I–II, 94.3 ad 2 and 3; II–II, 57.2 ad 2, 64.5, 66.7, 78.1 ad 3, 81.2 ad 3, 88.3 ad 1, and 88.10 ad 2).

There is an interesting problem here: Sigmund's rather short list of prescriptions and duties notes the behavior that Thomas held to be, in some sense, contrary to or in accord with natural law, but anyone explicating Thomas's theory faces the challenge of demonstrating the extent to which Thomas delivers on natural law's promise to tell us how to live. It does seem at least problematic that Thomas neglected to provide a more extensive or coherently organized listing of natural-law verdicts. Even supposing that the moral judgments cataloged in lists like Sigmund's are best interpreted as straightforward natural-law deductions, one still wonders how the specific judgments on the list are related to the totality of natural law. One solution, discussed below in more detail, is to claim that natural law contains only a few very general judgments. The difficulty with such a proposal is that it minimizes the epistemic importance and practical usefulness of natural law, emptying the theory of meaningful content and locating the resources for specific moral decision making elsewhere. The other main alternative is to claim that even specific moral judgments are contained in the natural law, but then Thomas provides unexpectedly little help in the way of examples or explicit method.

It should not be surprising, therefore, that many of Thomas Aquinas's successors and modern commentators say either more or less than did Thomas about the specific content of the natural law. There is a temptation to say *less* because Thomas nowhere provides a complete or detailed enumeration of what one might suppose are the actual precepts of the natural law. He does say *something* about its content, however, which apparently leads some interpreters to avoid altogether the difficult task of actually listing the precepts: Any sustained discussion of the specific principles of the law of nature according to St. Thomas in sufficient detail to constitute an adequate moral code requires more evidence than the texts provide. On the other hand, there is a temptation to say *more:* Many of Thomas's interpreters discern within his references to natural law hints of a methodology supposedly sufficient to elaborate the missing precepts of the legal system in a manner faithful to the spirit, although unfortunately not the exact words, of St. Thomas.

However the various precepts of the natural law are enumerated, and however their derivation from the first principle is explained, it is common to discuss their application to concrete moral problems and questions in terms of the practical syllogism, a form of reasoning in which conclusions are derived from general major premises via more specific minor premises. This characterization of the "core" of Thomas's ethics lends to Thomistic natural law a particularly deductive appearance and the suggestion that it claims the formulaic certainty of logic.

Some commentators, however, qualify their claims about the certainty of natural law, accurately noting that St. Thomas, in fact, distinguishes between two kinds of syllogistic reasoning: There are scientific syllogisms, which are certain in that the conclusions follow from necessarily true premises, and dialectical syllogisms, which are only probable in their conclusions (O'Connor 1967: 10). (Interpreters who fail to appreciate this distinction tend to presume "scientific" certainty for the latter kind of reasoning.) While the major premise in a practical syllogism, stating that some kind of action is right or wrong, is alleged to be necessarily true since it is given by synderesis, there is room for error in the minor premise, which says that some specific action is an instance of the general kind of action identified in the major premise as good or evil. Consequently, the judgment expressed in the conclusion, that the concrete action specified in minor premise should or should not be done, cannot be absolutely certain although it is nonetheless binding on conscience (1967: 42–43).

One important way in which my interpretation of Thomas differs from the standard reading concerns the question of how to understand the significance of Thomas's use of syllogisms. If one approaches the texts anticipating the usual more or less deductive version of syllogistic natural-law reasoning, Thomas's syllogizing certainly seems to confirm the usual interpretive presuppositions. If those presuppositions are suspended, however, there is at least the possibility of another interpretation of the force of the syllogistic arguments. The question I raise concerns the epistemic status of the syllogisms. The standard interpretation appeals to the intuitive certainty of the premises, clothing the syllogism in the authority of natural law. My interpretation, on the other hand, sees Thomas's premises as derived primarily from the kind of prudential judgments made by virtuous individuals drawing on the moral resources and experience of a community and a tradition.

In contrast to the interpretation that I propose, the role given to prudence and the virtues in the standard account is minor compared to the status accorded synderesis and the judgments obtained by employing the practical syllogism. Even in a recent study that emphasizes the generality and vagueness of natural-law judgments derived from natural inclinations, and which stresses prudence's function of deciding here and now what is to be done in questions of moral choice, prudence still is placed in the service of natural law, on which it depends: "The sequence of stages in practical knowledge can . . . be summarized as beginning in the Eternal Law, passing to the natural law and thence to the concrete recommendations of prudence" (Spinnenweber 1972: 13).

Spinnenweber points out that the moral virtues are guides for prudence in its task of finding the right means to ends of human action, that prudence is involved in every choice of means, and that "genuinely prudent choice is possible only for man of solid moral virtue" (1972: 221–28). Nevertheless, he adds that "prudence does not provide man with profound moral insight, but is concerned with the moment to moment choices directed to an end which it does not question but assumes" (1972: 229). Prudence depends on conscience, which he describes as moral ability in action, and conscience depends on *synderesis* for the first step in moral reasoning, the apprehension of "foundational truths" (1972: 300, 307).

Another, more common, approach is to associate all moral knowledge with the natural law, to assign prudence the task of applying that independently derived knowledge to concrete cases, and then to attribute to the other moral virtues the responsibility for motivating correct behavior. According to Higgins, who employs these distinctions, the "science of ethics" provides an account of the moral laws that can be deduced from

the first principles of the natural law. The goal of the science is to produce
an upright character through the exercise of virtuous traits (1958: 147,
168).

Modern critics of Thomistic ethics commonly direct their objections to
variations on the standard version of natural law just sketched. Part of the
argument of this study is that whatever the force of the objections, they
apply to a particularly widespread interpretation of Thomas, but not
necessarily to an interpretation in which the epistemic role of natural law
is minimized. In other words, modern philosophical evaluations of Thomas,
which treat him as a representative of a disproven moral theory and
therefore as having only historical interest, have quite possibly rejected an
inauthentic Thomas Aquinas.

D. J. O'Connor, a rather sympathetic critic, whose interpretation of
Thomas was in keeping with the philosophical preoccupations of the
times by stressing Thomas's allegedly "adept" but futile attempt to derive
judgments of value from factual judgments about the essence of human
nature (1967: 61, 68) is a case in point. He argues that Thomistic natural
law fails to survive at least four important criticisms: (1) If the primary
precepts are intuitively known, Thomas is subject to well-established
objections to moral intuitionism. (2) Even if there is such a thing as an
essential human nature, Thomas is guilty of committing the "naturalistic
fallacy" by attempting to derive what ought to be (values) from what is
(facts). (3) Thomas nowhere adequately describes or defends the derivation of secondary precepts from primary precepts of natural law (those
that are less immediately known from those that are known most
immediately). (4) Thomas's acknowledgment of the natural law's variabil-
ity is in tension with other claims about its absolute and universal status.
(All of these objections are discussed in O'Connor, 1967, especially
64–79.)

                                        V

Rather than casting about for defenses of Thomistic natural law against a
representative array of modern criticisms, thereby taking this study into
the thicket (from which it would be a long time emerging) of contemporary discussion of the so-called naturalistic fallacy, I propose to focus on

the particular question of the relation between natural law's primary and secondary principles. The discussion of how the secondary principles are derived permeates the literature and provides a useful insight into the structure and operation of the standard Thomistic version of natural law in general. Differences of opinion on this question are an instance of the diversity within the standard account. Almost everyone agrees it is an important problem, but there is considerable disagreement about whether or how Thomas provides a solution.

The 1966 study by R. A. Armstrong is a helpful reference at this point, but not because of its wide influence or because his interpretation of Thomas is especially compelling or provocative. Armstrong's analysis is convenient because his reading of Thomas closely approximates what I have been calling the standard account, departing from it only in details, and because his study is recent and thorough enough to survey most of the other important modern explications. Armstrong's study has the additional virtues of treating all of Thomas's relevant texts chronologically (many commentators treat Thomas's work as a seamless and timeless whole) and of carefully documenting Thomas's teaching about natural law while staying close to the texts, refraining from introducing extraneous supportive material "in the spirit of the Angelic Doctor." The ambiguities in his analysis of how more specific moral judgments are obtained from the most general primary principles of natural law tend to mirror ambiguities in the standard account.

Armstrong distinguishes among writers claiming the authority of Thomas who make three distinct general claims about the kinds of precepts that make up the natural law. (In his discussion, the terms "principles" and "precepts" are used interchangeably.) According to the first group, the entirety of the natural law is restricted to a few general and changeless principles (1966: 1-7; Edgar Janssens, *Cours de morale generale*, 1926, is representative of this first group). The second reading, defended by Jacques Maritain, says that both general principles as well as more specific secondary principles are contained in the natural law and that both kinds of principles are invariable. In Maritain's words, "Natural law is coextensive with the whole field of natural moral regulations, of natural morality. Not only the primary and fundamental precepts but the remotest regulations of natural ethics means conformity to natural law" (*Man and the State*, 1954; quoted by Armstrong 1966: 10-14). The third position, closest to Armstrong's own reading, has it that both primary and secondary precepts make up the natural law, but the primary principles are changeless while the secondary precepts may vary (1966: 14–21; see also Odon Lottin, *Le droit naturel chez S. Thomas et ses predecesseurs,* 1931, and Heinrich Rommen, *Die ewige Wiederkehr des Naturrechts,* 1936, translated by T. R. Hanley as *The Natural Law,* 1947).

Another distinction between primary and secondary principles, according to Armstrong's explication, is that the former are self-evident. A note of caution at this point: "Self-evident" is the usual translation of Thomas's term *"per se nota,"* but this is a rough, and sometimes misleading, rendering. Victor Preller's warning is worth heeding: "Aquinas' use of *'per se nota'* cannot be comprehended if 'self-evident' is our *only* translation of the phrase. A literal translation is more informative: a *per se nota* proposition is a proposition whose truth is *known through itself* and not *per aliud* or *through another*" (Preller 1967: 82; emphasis in the original).

Armstrong says that Thomas's early claim in the *Commentary* and in *De veritate,* substantially unchanged in the *Summa* except for an apparent reluctance to make as much use of the term *synderesis,* is that practical reason possesses several self-evident and general primary principles, analogous to the first principles of speculative reason, which are not innate but whose truth is immediately known once one is familiar with the requisite terms. These first principles are further distinguished in that one's knowledge of them is always accurate, although they may not always be applied accurately (1966: 25–35; citing Peter Lombard's *Sentences,* d. 39, q. 3, a.1; and *De Veritate,* q. 16, a. 1–3). Thomas also distinguishes between two ways in which first principles are self-evident, he adds. Some are self-evident to every rational person while others, although evident in themselves, are only apprehended by individuals of sufficient wisdom or experience. That is, in both cases the self-evidence of the principles depends on knowledge of the terms involved, but in the latter case the terms are more complex than in the former (1966: 35–37; who cites *S.T.* I–II, q. 94, a. 2–4).

Armstrong denies that Thomas held the very first principle of practical reason — good is to be pursued and evil avoided — to be one from which all other principles could be straightforwardly deduced. Rather, it "has the status of a *directive principle* — it is in accord with this principle that all precepts of the natural law must be formulated" (1966: 40; emphasis in the original). This first principle is self-evident to everyone, but there are additional principles which are also self-evident in themselves, although not to all (1966: 40).

The way the primary precepts, which are self-evident in themselves, are apprehended by those capable of understanding the terms involved, Armstrong explains, is by way of the natural inclinations, and the way to compile a list of the first principles of natural law is to list the corresponding inclinations (1966: 48). (Armstrong accepts Thomas's account of the natural inclinations without discussion, although a critic would certainly wish to see the list defended.) Associated with the inclination to self-preservation is the principle, summarized by Armstrong, that "while recognizing that not all beings have equal value in the world of creation, one ought to respect and preserve not only human life, but where possible, all life" (1966: 48). The natural desire for sexual intercourse and to raise children corresponds with the natural-law precepts stating that sexual and family relationships need order and regulation (1966: 48). Armstrong denies that there are any self-evident principles associated with the inclination to know the truth about God, but says that the human inclination to live with others in society has associated with it the fundamental principle that "we ought to live together in obedience to certain rules" (1966: 49–50).

Thomas's teaching prior to the *Summa* occasionally distinguished between primary and secondary precepts by referring to the primary ends of actions: "[A]n action was against the primary precepts of the natural law, if it in any way prevented an action's primary end, while an action was contrary to the secondary precepts of the natural law if the action in question either hindered the realization of the primary end of the action, or totally prevented or hindered the secondary end of an action [Suppl. 65.1]" (Armstrong 1966: 69). On other occasions, however, he followed an approach more continuous with the teaching in the *Summa,* distinguishing the primary precepts as self-evident and the secondary precepts as those that somehow follow from them (Armstrong 1966: 69; Suppl. 65.2).

Thomas's mature position in the *Summa,* Armstrong claims, is that the secondary precepts are not actually deduced from primary precepts but are "proximate" to them. A proximate precept is one that is "closely derived" from a primary precept. Describing how this process of derivation works, Armstrong says that if "we were to place the primary precept 'respect the lawful rights of others' [already apparently a derivation from the even more primary precept "we ought to live together in obedience to certain rules"] alongside the more particular precept 'do not steal what belongs to others,' we can see almost immediately that the latter precept follows from the former." In general, primary precepts are more abstract than secondary precepts, which concern concrete and contingent particulars of life. The more specific the situation, the more details and circumstances have to be considered in order to determine the judgment of natural law (Armstrong 1966: 92–93). In fact, Armstrong says that for Thomas, *every* moral judgment is a natural-law judgment: "[A]ll moral precepts whose truth is able to be assented to by the *ratio naturalis* of man (even though some might require more sustained reflection than others) are part of the content of the natural law" (1966: 104).

Distinguished within Thomas's teaching on natural law, then, are very general primary precepts, which are *per se nota,* slightly more specific secondary precepts, which are "known almost immediately after knowing the truth of the primary precepts," and more remote conclusions, which, although still part of natural law, "can only be assented to after considerable reflection" (Armstrong 1966: 106–7).

One of the difficulties with Armstrong's study is that he seems to be of two minds about the relationship between primary and secondary precepts. Although he sometimes resists the notion that secondary precepts are deduced from primary or self-evident precepts, at other times he subscribes to the deductive account. For example, at one point Armstrong insists that knowledge of first principles is not adequate for moral choice, and that a process of prudential reasoning is required for an appreciation of the truth of the so-called secondary precepts. To accept the truth of the injunction against stealing, he points out, one requires more than knowledge of the first principle that "we ought to live together in society under certain rules." Beyond this general sort of knowledge, which is insufficient for decision making, one also must "reflect on what is required by the common good as it is manifested in the rights of property" (1966: 127).

At other points, however, the deductive version is predominant. The secondary precepts contained in the decalogue, for example, are "not self-evident, but require to be drawn from general precepts in the manner of conclusions" (Armstrong 1966: 111). He also expresses cautious agreement with a statement by D'Arcy that "[t]he principles given by *synderesis* are rather like axioms from which, theorem-like, moral principles are deduced with greater or less facility" (D'Arcy, 1961: 60; quoted by Armstrong 1966: 129). And when he describes how secondary precepts come to be formulated, he employs the following example of the formulation of the precept requiring monogamous sexual relations: One starts with the first principle, which states that sexual relations ought to be regulated. Citing the difficulty of determining paternity under nonmonogamous forms of sexual relation, Armstrong says that "[w]e need only to reflect on experience to see that *it follows from this* [first] *principle* that a woman should only have one husband at a time. . . . When we apply this thinking to the self-evident principle stated above, *we are able to derive a conclusion* of the kind . . . 'polyandrous [and polygamous] unions are contrary to the natural law.'" He concludes that "[t]his same method of approach can also be applied with regard to the other self-evident principles, and in this way additional natural-law precepts will come to be formulated" (Armstrong 1966: 129–30; emphasis added).

VI

Armstrong's account, despite the attempt to clarify the relation between primary and secondary principles, is unlikely to satisfy a critic who might well maintain that none of the variations on the standard version of Thomistic natural law escapes potentially devastating philosophical objections. I have no direct interest in attempting to defend the naturallaw tradition against the sorts of criticisms noted by O'Connor (above), but neither do I see any compelling reason to set much store in the supposed force of the critics' favorite objection, that Thomas and his heirs had committed the so-called naturalistic fallacy. As I have already noted, the pursuit of that issue is beyond the scope of this study. I mention it again in passing only because it is taken so seriously by John Finnis (1980), who acknowledges its force but denies that Thomas's understanding of natural law is vulnerable. Finnis is pertinent to this study, although not because of his response to the is/ought problem. Finnis is one of those, on the margins of the tradition, who shares the assumption that Thomas is articulating a doctrine of natural law, but whose reading of it differs markedly from the standard accounts in ways that Finnis thinks preserve Thomas's contemporary relevance. He claims

> a theory of practical reasonableness, of forms of human good, and of practical principles, such as the theory Aquinas adumbrated but left insufficiently elaborated, is untouched by the objections which Hume (and after him the whole Enlightenment and post-Enlightenment current of ethics) was able to raise against the

tradition of rationalism eked out by voluntarism. That tradition
presented itself as the classical or central tradition of natural law
theorizing, but in truth it was peculiar to late scholasticism. . . . The
substantive differences between the theory of natural law espoused
by Vázquez and Suárez (and most Catholic manuals until the
other day) and the theory espoused by Aquinas are scarcely less
significant and extensive than the better-known differences between
Aristotelian and Stoic ethics. But ecclesiastical deference to a
misread Aquinas obscured the former differences until well into
this century. (Finnis 1980: 46–47)

Finnis shares MacIntyre's general doubts about attributing the naturalistic-
fallacy argument to Hume. His reasons are worth noting here because
of their connection with at least one explanation for how the Thomas
that Finnis discerns came to be displaced by the Thomas of the dis-
credited or refuted natural-law tradition. I should say now that Finnis's
Thomas is not the Thomas I shall be describing in Chapter 2, but I share
Finnis's mistrust of the identity of the established Thomas. On Finnis's
account, a reading of David Hume's famous objection (at III.I.i of *A
Treatise of Human Nature*) in its textual and historical context suggests it
was most likely not directed against the leap from factual to evaluative
claims. Rather, it was directed against the jump from any truth claim
to claims about motivation. The specific target, according to Finnis (42),
was Samuel Clarke's attempt in *A Discourse Concerning the Unchangeable Obligations of Natural Religion* (1706, eighth edition, 1732) "to
show that moral truths provide a (conclusive) reason for action." Whatever the proper interpretation of Hume's objection (and Finnis accepts
the force of both renderings, regardless of the version for which Hume
deserves credit), Finnis says that the significance of Hume's attack on
Clarke is that it ended 150 years of development of natural-law theory
(1980: 42). Moreover, since Hume supposedly refuted the central claims
of the theory, then Thomas Aquinas as the foremost figure within the
tradition has had only historical interest for most of modern moral
philosophy.

The chain of connections between the position refuted by Hume and
Thomas's authentic position extends back from Clarke through Grotius,
Suárez, and Vázquez, according to Finnis. He says that Grotius raised this
problem, addressed by Clarke: If human reason is able to distinguish right
from wrong, why is reason obliged to choose the right? The standard

answer was that the determination of right and wrong was to be made by reference to nature (independent of divine legislation), but that moral obligation depended on an expression of God's will. Clarke's view differed on this point and was especially vulnerable because he tried to make obligation to do the right, as well as knowledge of the right, a matter of conformity to nature (Finnis 1980: 44–45).

Vázquez and Suárez, Grotius's predecessors, differed from Thomas, Finnis claims, on both counts. That is, first, their version of natural law held that reason's crucial role is to perceive whether or not a given action is "fitting" to rational human nature and therefore to be pursued or avoided. In contrast, Finnis says, Thomas's understanding of natural law depended on "one's understanding of the basic forms of (not-yet-moral) human well-being as desirable and potentially realizable ends or opportunities and thus to be pursued and realized in one's action" (1980: 45). Second, obligation for Suárez and Vázquez seems to depend on the act of a superior's will, while for Thomas obligation has to do with "the rational necessity of some means to (or way of realizing) an end or objective (i.e. a good)" related to human well-being (1980: 45–46).

On this basis, Finnis presents a reading of Aquinas and an account of natural law indebted to him that claims to be untouched by the usual criticisms. Finnis attempts to derive principles of natural law by applying "first principles of practical reasonableness" to certain basic "pre-moral goods." The significance, for this discussion, of Finnis's natural-law theory is his departure from the standard account in arguing that moral laws are *not* deduced from human nature: "[F]or Aquinas, the way to discover what is morally right (virtue) and wrong (vice) is to ask, not what is in accordance with human nature, but what is reasonable. And this quest will eventually bring one back to the *underived* first principles of practical reasonableness, principles which make no reference at all to human nature but only to human good" (1980: 36).

The appeal to some alternative version of practical reason is an attractive way out of some of the difficulties encountered by the standard versions of Thomas's ethics—attractive because of support within the texts themselves and because the ordinary criticisms are not applicable. Nonetheless, Finnis's presuppositions about human reason and the nature of ethics lead him to retain much of the natural law vocabulary. His reading challenges an important part of the traditional methodology, but not the theory's larger claims. A critique of Finnis might profitably begin by examining the evidence for the support Finnis finds in Thomas for his own version of natural law. Then it would be well to inquire, regardless of the extent to which Finnis and Thomas overlap, about the usefulness of Finnis's proposal and to ask whether or not the very notion of natural law requires an understanding of human reason that we have reasons to abandon. This essay's more pressing task, however, is to proceed toward the discussion of an interpretation of Thomas's ethics that finds him relying on a version of practical reason rooted in the tradition of the virtues.

This essay began by reviewing the familiar narrative of the natural-law tradition and St. Thomas's customary place of honor within it. The next step was a summary of the standard account of the Thomistic doctrine of natural law. That portrayal acknowledged the diversity within the standard account but also recognized the broad agreement behind the variety of interpretations. The standard account is something about which critics and defenders of Thomistic natural law tend to agree, and one of the features that makes it standard is agreement about the kind of problems that the theory encounters. Many more detailed discussions of the standard account already exist. For my purposes, it is only necessary to highlight the conventional reading so my interpretation might be more readily distinguished from it. Finally, I acknowledge that the standard account, however dominant, is not the only rendition. I introduced John Finnis's demurral, worth discussion in its own right, as an illustration of this complexity. Finnis's response to the objections facing natural law is to redefine it in a way that he finds fortuitously suggested by St. Thomas. But neither Finnis nor others, such as Karl Rahner, who attempts to supplement natural law with another kind of moral decision making that he says is inspired by Thomas, have completely broken with the natural-law tradition, perhaps because they have not pursued Thomas's use of prudence far enough to escape the shadow of the St. Thomas in the standard account.

2

THE CONTEXT FOR PRUDENCE

God as the universal mover moves the will of man to the univer-
sal object of the will, which is the good. Without this universal
motion man cannot will anything. But man by his reason deter-
mines himself to will this or that thing, which is either a true good
or an apparent good.
                                                          —*Summa Theologica*

Reason's decision or judgment of what is to be done is about
contingent matters which can be done by us. In these matters,
conclusions do not necessarily follow from necessary principles
with absolute necessity, but only conditionally.
                                                          —*Summa Theologica*

I

In this chapter I intend to begin delivery on the promise to provide
reasons and evidence for saying it is a mistake to understand Thomas's
moral teaching primarily in terms of natural law. A rich enough description of prudence and its role in practical reason should make plausible
my claim that Thomas's ethics depend more on prudential than natural-
law reasoning. Incidentally, I hope that the description, in this chapter
and the next, of the components of the virtue and the spheres in which
prudence operates will help to rehabilitate it for contemporary discussion
and cultivation. Rather than jumping directly to Thomas's explicit treatment of prudence, however, we first need to consider the view of human
agency and the moral analysis of human acts that forms the context for
prudence and the other cardinal virtues.

My main source will be the *Prima Secundae*, the first of two sections of
the second part of the *Summa Theologica*, which contains Thomas's
general account of the virtues. Because the *Summa* was written late in
Thomas's career, it is reasonable to suppose that the teaching contained
within it represents his mature position. Moreover, Thomas says it was
written for beginners in theology. This is not to claim it is an easy book,

but that it can plausibly be understood as an attempt to articulate the fundamentals of theology and ethics.

The standard natural-law interpretation of Thomas also relies primarily on the second part of the *Summa*. One explanation for how two very different accounts of Thomas's ethics can claim support from the same source is that it has been a common practice to read individual segments or treatises within the *Summa* in isolation, paying scant attention to Thomas's order of presentation or to the context of a larger discussion in which a particular sequence of questions is imbedded. The conventional division of the work into treatises and the detailed outlines that have been made of the various divisions permit convenient reference but also make it easy to avoid confronting the *Summa* as a whole.

Whatever the reasons for why Thomas has been read as the authoritative natural-law theorist, that interpretation is easily perpetuated by presenting the "Treatise on Law" as the crux of his moral teaching. Readers wishing a quick and easy introduction to Thomas's ethics often read the treatise, or excerpts from it, without any awareness of the preceding material. The expectation of finding a doctrine of natural law is confirmed when the one question (*S.T.* I–II, q. 94) specifically about natural law, which occurs within the larger discussion of law in general and is located at the tail end of the *Prima Secundae*, is used as the key to understanding Thomas's ethics. The more responsible approach is to follow the sequence of Thomas's own presentation and to acknowledge the content of the discussion preceding the treatment of natural law.

My discussion in these next two chapters has little to say about prudence *per se* that has not already been said in other treatments of the *Summa*. What is new is the relative importance of the virtues in general, and the virtue of prudence in particular, that becomes evident when the natural-law schema for interpretation is suspended and one begins the consideration of ethics where Thomas does, rather than with his discussion of law. I am not claiming that the text will somehow speak for itself if we will but abandon all our presuppositions. I am bringing my own questions and concerns to the text, and it would be a mistake to feign an unachievable neutrality. By bringing new questions to the text, however, it is possible to discover that the text has something more to offer than previously supposed. The conventional interpretation of Thomas is so well established that readers sharing its presuppositions are protected from being challenged by what he has to say. As readers, we should not presume or pretend to abandon completely our own points of view, but we should try to read in a way that permits our acknowledged perspectives on the text to be called into question. Asking whether Thomas understands the virtues and especially prudence as more than a mere adjunct to a natural-law ethics is a strategy for making our understanding vulnerable once again to an all-too-familiar text. Obviously, one does not bring just any question to the text. One makes educated guesses about the kind of questioning that might be productive. There already is enough attention paid to the virtues in the standard interpretation, and enough dissent about the standard emphasis on law, to suggest that questioning about the role of prudence is appropriate.

This chapter's claim, then, is that by following the sequence of Thomas's own presentation of the relevant material, and by placing his discussions of prudence and natural law in the larger context of the *Prima Secundae,* a picture of practical reasoning emerges in which prudence and not natural law is central. Thomas himself provides a warrant for relying primarily on the *Summa* and for carefully attending to his overall arrangement of its content. In his short prologue to the entire work he says: "[W]e propose in this book to treat of whatever belongs to the Christian Religion, in such a way as may tend to the instruction of beginners. We have considered that students in this Science have not seldom been hampered by what they have found written by other authors, partly on account of the multiplication of useless questions, articles, and arguments; partly also because those things that are needful for them to know are not taught according to the order of their subject-matter" (1947: *S.T.* Prologue, xxi). An adequate discussion of how the entire *Summa* forms the context for the discussion of ethics is certainly beyond the scope of this study, but as an introduction to Thomas's treatment of ethics it is possible briefly to review the arrangement of the contents and then to describe in more detail the questions with which Thomas is concerned in the *Prima Secundae* prior to his discussion of the virtues and law.

The theological themes of *exitus* and *reditus* underlie the division of the *Summa* into its three main parts. The first part has to do with God and the "procession" of creation from God. The second part, the richest source for Thomas's specifically ethical teaching, concerns the return of rational creatures to God. The first part of the second part, the *Prima Secundae,* is a moral analysis of human acts and a general discussion of passions, habits and virtues, sin, law, and grace. A more detailed discussion of specific virtues occupies the *Secunda Secundae.* Christ, who brings us to God, is the subject of the third part.

In keeping with the disputational manner of intellectual inquiry standard in Thomas's time, each part of the *Summa* is organized into a series of questions identifying a general topic, and each question is further divided into a number of articles, or more specific points of inquiry, pertaining to the topic. An article begins by asking a question about the general topic and by presenting a number of arguments or "objections" contrary to the position defended by Thomas. The transition to Thomas's reply to the objections is the *sed contra,* a brief section introduced by the phrase translated as "On the other hand" or "On the contrary," where Thomas often cites scripture or some authority (frequently Aristotle) against the objection. Thomas's own position is defended by argument in the sometimes lengthy reply. The article concludes with specific responses to the individual objections raised at the beginning. It is worth remembering that the question encompassing each article, and the specific contrary position and objections to which Thomas is responding within an article, constitute a context that can profoundly affect the interpretation of Thomas's teaching. It is also worth noting that Thomas's position on a topic is frequently developed over a series of articles and questions. Thus, to read passages in isolation or out of context can be to misread them.

The first part of the *Summa* begins with a question on "The Nature and Extent of Sacred Doctrine," establishing the purview of theology, and moves immediately, in questions 2 through 43, to a discussion of the attributes of God, the persons of the Trinity, and their relations. This introductory section is followed by the "Treatise on Creation" (qq. 44–49), the "Treatise on Angels" (qq. 50–64), and the "Treatise on the Work of the Six Days" (qq. 65–74). The "Treatise on Man" (qq. 75–102) discusses humans as corporeal and spiritual beings, describes human intellectual and appetitive powers as well as human knowledge, and concludes with a description of humans as created beings.

The *Prima Secundae*, the first half of the second part, is profoundly theological in its explicit treatment of ethics. The material contained within it presupposes the preceding discussion of the emanation of creation from God. Contrary to what one might expect of a treatise on ethics by a supposed natural lawyer, it does not begin with a discussion of moral law but rather with a discussion (qq. 1–5) of the last end of humanity and of human happiness, the beatific vision of God. The account in questions 6 through 17 of what constitutes morally significant, and therefore truly human, action—its voluntary nature, the significance of circumstances, and the orientation of the will—depends on the prior portrayal of God's creation of humans as creatures capable of reason and choice. Thomas then advances to a discussion of the way in which human acts in general and acts of the will in particular can be described as good or evil (qq. 18-21). The lengthy discussion of human passions (qq. 22-48) immediately precedes the "Treatise on Habits" (qq. 49-69).

The first section of that treatise (qq. 49-54) concerns the substance, subject, formation, increase, diminution, and distinction of habits in general. The next section (qq. 55-67) concerns specific kinds of habits, the virtues. Thomas treats the essence and subject of virtues; the distinction between moral and intellectual virtues; the relation between specific moral virtues and the passions; how individual moral virtues differ; cardinal and theological virtues; the cause, "mean," interconnection, and equality of the virtues; and the duration of the virtues after death. Questions 68 through 70 concern spiritual gifts, beatitudes, and the fruits of the Holy Spirit. Questions 71 through 89 are about vice and sin: the distinction, comparison, subject, and causes of sin; original sin; the consequences of sin; and the distinction between venial and mortal sin.

The "Treatise on Law" (qq. 90-114) occurs near the very end of the *Prima Secundae*. The overall sequence is instructive. To review, Thomas, following Aristotle, commences the treatment of ethics by talking about the end of human action, happiness. He then moves to an analysis of human will and how we are moved by passions. Next, he discusses habits in general and virtues in particular. Finally, after an extensive discussion of sin, he takes up the subject of law. After describing the essence, various kinds, and effects of law (qq. 90-92), he addresses the topic of eternal law in question 93 and the natural law in question 94. The next three questions (95-97) are concerned with human law. The bulk of the treatise (qq. 98-108) has to do with the old and new law of the Bible. The treatise concludes with six questions (109-14) on the topic of grace. Thomas's major discussion of ethics, in other words, neither begins with nor culminates in a discussion of natural law, a topic to which he devotes the entirety of only one question.

Thomas introduces the *Prima Secundae* by saying "now that we have treated of the exemplar, *i.e.*, God, and of those things which came forth from the power of God in accordance with his will; it remains for us to treat of his image, *i.e.*, man, inasmuch as he too is the principle of his actions, as having free-will and control of his actions" (I-II, Prologue). Set in the theological context established by the first and third parts of the *Summa*, the *Prima Secundae* itself begins and ends its moral analysis of human action on theological notes: God as the true end and ultimate happiness of humanity and the necessity of grace for achieving that end. At least on the basis of a surface description of its contents and order of presentation, the *Prima Secundae* does not appear to be primarily concerned with conveying or defending a doctrine of natural law. So far, the most that can be said is that it provides an account of virtue and vice as what Thomas calls the "intrinsic principles" of human action and of law and grace as human action's "extrinsic principles." In order to judge the relative importance of those principles for moral decision making we need to consider Thomas's discussion of the morality of human action in more detail. My objective in this endeavor is not to provide anything like a complete recapitulation, but to follow Thomas's own order of discussion and to put forth and interpret what particularly pertains to the question of whether his ethics are primarily prudential or grounded in natural law.

II

Thomas's discussion of the virtues and of law occurs near the end of the *Prima Secundae*. In order properly to understand him, we cannot begin where he concludes but where he begins, with a discussion of what ethics is about. My concern in starting at the beginning is neither to summarize nor to defend the entirety of what Thomas says about the scope of ethics, but rather to present the features of Thomas's preliminary discussion that illuminate the question of the relative importance of prudence or natural law in moral reasoning.

The first thing to note about Thomas's characterization of ethics is that his account of the moral life is both teleological and eudaemonistic. That is, he follows Aristotle in affirming that our actions and lives are oriented to an end and that there is a connection between the kind of action characteristic of a good life and happiness. Thomas elaborates this view on two levels, the first having to do with the general features of human action and the second concerning a specific theological claim.

He begins the *Prima Secundae* by affirming Aristotle's claim that all human action is for the sake of an end and by stating that what makes actions truly human and therefore morally significant, as opposed to being merely "actions of a man," is the fact that they are "deliberately willed" in view of an end (1963: *S.T.* I–II, q. 1, a. 1; subsequent references to the "Treatise on Happiness" will be to this translation). Morality has to do with the actions of rational creatures, who are distinguished from animals in having this ability to direct their own actions toward an end through their powers of will and reason (ibid., a. 2). Any end that we will, Thomas claims, is willed because we apprehend it as good. To say that we act for the sake of an end is to say that we act for the sake of something that seems good to us (ibid., a. 3).

Thomas also affirms that humans have a distinct *telos,* a specific end, purpose, or final good, the achievement of which constitutes their happiness. He says that there is, in fact, an *ultimate* end (ibid., a. 4) which, because it is ultimate, is necessarily a single end (ibid., a. 5) and necessarily the end for the sake of which every other end is desired (ibid., a. 6). This view presumes that there is a distinct human nature. Humans, like every other creature or thing, have a nature with a particular end or *telos.* Just as a good saw is one that achieves the end of cutting well, a good person is one who successfully achieves the end appropriate to human nature, whatever that might turn out to be. So far, this is a straightforwardly Aristotelian argument that will assume a theological cast only when Thomas claims that our ultimate end, true good, and final happiness is to be found in God (q. 3, a. 8). What is immediately important here, however, is that he has oriented his discussion in a way that will permit him to argue that there is a way of life particularly appropriate to humans. If there is an ultimate end, a life successfully lived in a way that is ordered to that end will lead to fulfillment, satisfaction of desires, the realization of the good we are aiming at, and the achievement of our ultimate happiness.

The problem is that we disagree about which ends are good. Moral disagreement reflects the fact that our apprehensions of the good differ. Most important, we lack agreement on what constitutes the ultimate end or good for which our nature is suited. Thomas's portrayal of this reality introduces a dominant theme in his thinking that is oriented to an ethics of virtue. Immediately after stating that every action can be referred to an ultimate end, he considers the proposition that everyone does not share the same ultimate end (q. 1, a. 7). In one respect everyone does agree on the ultimate end, he says, because everyone acts for the sake of an end apprehended as good. In fact, we act in order to achieve our complete good, which is what the ultimate end is. At that level of generality, for Thomas, there is no dispute. He then immediately acknowledges the lack of universal agreement about the nature of the ultimate good: "But with respect to that in which this kind of thing is realized, all men are not agreed as to their ultimate end, for some desire riches as their complete good, some sense pleasure, and others something else" (ibid.).

If Thomas were introducing an ethics of natural law, one would expect him at this point to provide an account of human nature to substantiate a claim about what the ultimate end is in truth. Instead, he resolves the problem of how to decide by asserting that "the most complete good absolutely must be what one *with well-disposed affections* desires for his ultimate end" (q. 1, a. 7; emphasis added). To have well-disposed affections, as we shall see, is to have one's will habituated in accord with virtue. In the very first question on the general topic of human action, Thomas strikingly affirms that the best available standard of judgment about the true nature of the ultimate good is the determination that would be made by an individual "well-disposed" to the good.

This claim, which seems to beg the question, is not even defended at this point but only illustrated with an analogy: Everyone likes the taste of something sweet, but not all agree on what sweet thing tastes the best. The way we decide, Thomas says, is by deferring to the judgment of the person with the best taste in such matters. This probably strikes most of us as odd. Despite our occasional deference to the judgments of experienced experts, for the most part we are inclined to think that disputes concerning matters of taste cannot be resolved. In fact, we use the phrase "a matter of taste" to cover a variety of questions concerning which we suppose one person's judgment to be as good as another's. Thomas, in contrast, supposes there is a fact of the matter and says that the question of what constitutes the ultimate end is like a matter of taste in which we ought to be guided by the person who has the best taste. The person qualified to know the ultimate end and good of human life, the person with the best taste for the good, is the person of virtue. As we shall see, Thomas will also use the prudential judgments made by a virtuous individual, rather than some account of human nature, as the standard for determining the goodness of subsidiary ends and the goodness of the means to achieve them.

So far, Thomas has made a number of related claims. He has described as morally significant and truly human those actions that are deliberately willed or directed towards an end. The reason our deliberate actions are morally significant is that the will's object is necessarily an end perceived as good, that every end we pursue is necessarily ordered to an ultimate end, and that there is a determinate ultimate end and complete good for humans. In article 8 of question 1 he equates that final end or universal good with happiness, "which all men desire." Particularly significant for this study is Thomas's insistence that there is an ultimate end, good, or happiness particularly suited for humans and his recognition of the lack of agreement about its nature. For Thomas, of course, the end that constitutes our true good and happiness is to be found in "knowing and loving God" (ibid.).

That theological claim is elaborated and restated in question 2, an investigation of where true happiness is to be found. He argues against the propositions that it consists in wealth, honors, fame, power, goods of the body or the soul, pleasure, or any created good (q. 2, aa. 1–8), notes in passing that happiness is the "true reward of virtue" (ibid., a. 2), and concludes, without argument, that God alone is the universal human good and ultimate happiness (ibid., a. 8). This theological assertion undeniably envelopes Thomas's teaching in the *Prima Secundae*, which begins by referring all of ethics to God as our true end and perfect happiness and which concludes with a discussion of God's grace as the necessary means for attaining that happiness. Nonetheless, much of Thomas's intermediate discussion is devoted to a discussion of what he calls imperfect happiness, the happiness that can be achieved in this life, and of the means by which it can be attained. The attainment of that kind of happiness, according to Thomas, is the concern of the practical activity of reason, the deliberation about our doing and making, about action. (The speculative activity of reason, in contrast, is about things that exist "out there" in the world, independently of our actions, and which are themselves the measure of truth.) Because our investigation is about how Thomas understands practical deliberation about action, whether he refers it to the activity of the virtue of prudence or to the apprehension of natural law by some function of conscience, we need to understand how Thomas understands the kind of happiness that is the object of our practical or moral deliberation.

We have already seen why acting in the right way is important to Thomas: The attainment of our true happiness depends on the direction of our will toward the authentically good ends ordered to our one ultimate end. Thomas's observation that happiness, perfect or imperfect, is essentially an activity reinforces that point and provides the transition to his account of the moral life sufficient for the happiness attainable in this world. Happiness is attained and constituted by a particular kind of activity. Although happiness is not merely the consequence or reward for acting in a particular way, but also consists in the activity itself, the causal connection between virtuous activity and happiness is entirely fitting, Thomas points out. Responding to the claim that happiness can be received from God in the absence of good deeds, he repeats that "happiness is obtained through action" and that a correctly ordered will is required in order to obtain the ultimate end, although he acknowledges that God conceivably could direct the will towards that end (q. 5, a. 7). It would be inappropriate, however, for a creature to obtain happiness apart from virtuous activity. Happiness is justly virtue's reward. The requirement for virtue preserves "the order in things" (ibid.).

At one level, Thomas's account of happiness is straightforwardly Aristotelian: Happiness is an "activity in accordance with complete virtue" (q. 3, a. 2). For Thomas, however, the kind of activity ultimately according with complete virtue and constituting perfect happiness is possible only in the next life and consists "in the vision of the divine essence" (ibid., a. 8). That vision is unattainable in this life. Because of the limiting conditions of human life, even the comparatively imperfect kind of activity of being joined with God that is possible cannot be continuously sustained. As a consequence, complete or perfect happiness is presently unattainable (ibid., a. 2).

The best kind of happiness that is available now is primarily the speculative activity of the intellect in contemplating God, but secondarily it consists "in the operation of the practical intellect directing human actions and passions, as is said in the [Nicomachean] Ethics [I, 13]" (ibid., a. 5). The practical intellect's operation of directing our actions and reactions may be a secondary kind of imperfect happiness, but it provides the focus for most of Thomas's subsequent discussion. Without minimizing Thomas's overarching theological claims about the activities of seeing and contemplating God, it is important to realize the implications of what Thomas is saying about this "secondary" dimension of the moral life. Investigation of the moral life, properly understood, is an investigation of a degree of our authentic happiness because living in the right way, or living virtuously, is what constitutes happiness.

Living virtuously, as we shall shortly see, implies far more for Thomas than it does for the modern understanding. We tend to think that the phrase "a virtuous life" is merely synonymous with "a moral life," where living the moral life is primarily a matter of somehow knowing right from wrong and then being motivated to do the right thing. According to

Thomas, a virtuous life refers immediately to the activity of specific virtues. Ethics, for Thomas, is only secondarily a matter of knowledge. Primarily, it is a matter of a life lived in a certain way. The activity characteristic of a life lived virtuously is itself the standard by which we come to obtain moral knowledge. Knowing how to act depends on following the example of someone who acts well. Moral wisdom is the result of experience in acting well. This is part of the sense in which the determination of the good is a matter of taste. Someone with a taste for the good, like someone with a developed taste for good wine, has perfected that capacity through practice, experience, and practical training. Knowledge of what is good is not fundamentally something intuited or learned through study but rather something obtained through activity. This will become more apparent as we follow Thomas's exposition. For now it is sufficient to see in what Thomas has said at least the suggestion of the possibility that the standard natural-law account, which begins with intuited moral knowledge and then proceeds to the virtues, has Thomas's conception reversed.

Thomas's discussion of the necessary conditions for the imperfect kind of happiness possible in this life is a brief and preliminary account of the necessary conditions for the flourishing of the virtues. In order to be happy, which is to say in order to be virtuous, "rectitude of the will" is required first of all (q. 4, a. 4). In addition, in order for a right will to succeed in achieving its proper ends, certain "external goods" are necessary. In order to live well, not only do we need the minimal means with which to subsist at all, but we require the means with which to do acts of virtue. These "[e]xternal goods are required for the imperfect happiness which can be had in this life," Thomas says, "not as being of the essence of happiness but as serving instrumentally for happiness, which consists in the activity of virtue." We need "bodily necessities both for the exercise of contemplative virtue and also for the exercise of practical virtue ... so as to perform the works of practical virtue" (q. 4, a. 7). (Incidentally, this position has profound implications for social policy and runs counter to a prevalent cultural presupposition that poverty *reflects* a lack of virtue. If Thomas is right, and if we want members of our community to be virtuous, we need to ask whether the economic structure is such that they have access to the material means of virtue.) Similarly, friends are an essential component of a person's happiness and virtue because they are necessary "for good activity, that is so that he may do good to them and delight in seeing them do good and be helped by them in doing his own good deeds. For, in order to do well, whether in the works of the active life or in the activity of the contemplative life, man needs the help of friends" (q. 4, a. 8).

When Thomas takes up the question of whether and how happiness is attained and lost, the discussion continues to presume the appropriateness of the vocabulary of virtue. The happiness of the active life can be lost when someone's will falls from virtue into vice, or when adverse circumstances inhibit the performance of virtuous acts (q. 5, a. 4). Although ultimate happiness cannot be attained through the exercise of an individual's natural powers, our present happiness can be so acquired, at least to a degree, as can virtue, the activity in which our happiness consists (ibid., aa. 5–6). Happiness, Thomas says, is obtained by and consists in a certain kind of activity: activity in accordance with virtue. In one sense, that is the same as saying that happiness is a matter of acting in accordance with human nature. The sense in which that is true is that we are beings whose nature is such that we find our true good and ultimate end in virtuous activity. Another sense in which that is true, as we shall see, is that happiness is a matter of acting in accordance with reason, because acting virtuously and acting reasonably will turn out to be equivalent, and because reason is the distinguishing feature of human nature. If Thomas were articulating the theory of natural law usually attributed to him, one might expect him at this point to provide the kind of description of human nature that would help to identify which activities in particular are appropriate. That is to say, if happiness is a matter of acting in accordance with nature it would seem that we need some specific information about human nature, beyond its orientation to virtue or reason in general, in order to know how to act in the sort of way conducive to happiness. Instead of doing that, Thomas proceeds in the opposite direction. He undertakes an analysis of human acts themselves, aimed at specifying the acts that lead to happiness and those that lead away from it.

Because properly human and morally significant acts are those that proceed from the rational appetite or will, he begins by discussing acts insofar as they are voluntary or involuntary and then considers their circumstances, the accidental factors pertaining to them that determine the way in which they are evaluated (q. 6, introduction). This suggests that in order to know how to be happy, in order to know how to act, we do not need to be concerned, at least first of all, with having speculative knowledge about the nature of the human species. What we need is practical knowledge about something very concrete, particular, and changeable: human acts and the circumstances that describe, locate, and distinguish them. As we shall see, this is precisely the concern of prudence.

The discussion of acts as voluntary or involuntary serves in part to preserve grounds for making moral judgments. If God, for example, were the immediate principle of our actions, they could no longer be said to be authentically ours, and we could not be held responsible for them. Thomas therefore begins the analysis of acts by arguing that God's influence on action as an "extrinsic" principle does not neutralize the voluntary nature of an act prompted by the "intrinsic" principles of cognition and appetite (q. 6, a. 1). Because not every act of every creature is morally significant, but only those characteristic of a rational creature, Thomas distinguishes the imperfectly voluntary acts of children and irrational animals from the perfectly voluntary acts of adults. The acts with which Thomas is concerned follow "upon a perfect knowledge of the end; for, after grasping the end, a man, by deliberating about the end and the means to it, can be moved to attain the end or not" (a. 2). This statement about the kinds of acts that are morally significant is simultaneously a summary of Thomas's concern with moral agents.

What is morally significant about agents whose actions are subject to moral evaluation is their apprehension of ends, their deliberation about the means for attaining those ends, and their desire to attain them. In saying this, Thomas has really outlined the subject matter of ethics, the investigation of the conditions for the attainment of a level of our proper happiness, end, or good as humans. That investigation has to do with whether or not our acts are in accordance with virtue and with the way in which we apprehend ends and endeavor to attain them. In fact, these two concerns cannot be separated. They amount to the same thing. The way in which we judge and strive for ends is exactly what acting virtuously is about, and it is precisely the cardinal virtues of justice, temperance, and courage under the direction of prudence that make our acts accord with virtue.

The only kinds of acts that can be judged as morally good or evil, Thomas says, are those that are voluntary, those that are deliberately willed on the basis of an apprehended end. Our willing, then, has to be free from constraint if our actions are to be subject to moral evaluation. Thomas recognizes that the various bodily powers commanded by the will can be coerced, that we can be forced to do something against our will, but he insists that the will itself is immune to compulsion of its interior act of inclining to a perceived good (q. 6, a. 4). Although an external act, such as nodding the head or raising an arm, can be forced, we cannot be forced to consent to the external act. We are always free to refuse to acknowledge that a compelled external act is good. In Thomas's view, we cannot be made to will something against our will. The immediate importance of this position, of course, is that it further specifies the sphere of moral responsibility: Every act of the will is necessarily free, and every act that is willed is morally significant. There is another level at which this view is especially pertinent to this study: Thomas is also saying that although our will is necessarily ordered to the good in general, its inclination to specific goods is not determinate but rather indeterminate and a matter of individual responsibility.

This becomes apparent in his insistence that the will acts freely even in sinning. Sinning, according to an objection he considers, is a movement contrary to rational nature and therefore violent or compelled. Thomas replies, "What the will tends to in sinning, though evil and contrary to a rational nature, is nevertheless apprehended as good and suitable to nature insofar as it is suitable to man by reason of some pleasurable sensation or some bad habit" (q. 6, a. 4; reply to objection 3). The reference to nature here is not at all an appeal to a standard for determining what constitutes a sin; it is an oblique statement about sin in general. Sin and evil are contrary to rational nature because they are contrary to reason, which is to say they are opposed to virtue and therefore opposed to our proper good and happiness as rational creatures. What is noteworthy is Thomas's statement that sinful and evil ends are mistakenly apprehended as good because of a defect in a character corrupted by bad habits or vices. Likewise, virtuous and good ends are correctly apprehended as good because of the perfection of character by the virtues. It is a matter of one's character, one's good or bad habits, one's virtues or vices, whether one's apprehension of a good is correct. We are not automatically ordered to what is authentically good but only to what (rightly or wrongly) seems good.

The orientation of this entire discussion to the vocabulary of the virtues and vices is illustrated by Thomas's reply to an objection that the passions of fear and concupiscence do such violence to the will as to render its actions involuntary (q. 6, aa. 6-7). The reply anticipates Thomas's explicit discussion of the passions and the virtues in the questions immediately following the analysis of human acts, where he describes the way that the virtues govern the passions. The virtue of fortitude, for example, is concerned with the passion of fear, and the virtue of temperance pertains to the passion of desire, or concupiscence. An individual possessed of the virtues of fortitude and temperance is one who fears only the right things, in the right time and place, and to the appropriate degree, and whose desires for apprehended goods are also appropriately directed and moderated. Thomas says here that an act prompted by fear is actually more voluntary than involuntary insofar as one wills a particular act as good in order to escape an evil that one fears (q. 6, a. 6). An act done from concupiscence is even more voluntary (unless one is so consumed by desire as to be demented), he says. In the case of fear, one's orientation to the good is indirect. The agent sees an act done out of fear as good only because it avoids an evil. In the case of desire, however, one is acting directly on the basis of a good desired inordinately (q. 6, a. 7). Any act that we will, Thomas is saying, has moral significance, and he constantly refers the rightness of our acting and willing to the reasoned control of the virtues.

After having discussed the end of human action, which is happiness, and after having described human action as voluntary, Thomas next considers "the particular conditions" or "individual accidents of human acts," which he calls their circumstances (q. 7, a. 1). These are the exterior conditions surrounding an act that are "outside the substance of an act, and yet in some way affect the act" (ibid.). If they are "accidents," the question immediately arises of whether they are relevant to the concerns of the theologian (ibid., a. 2). Thomas gives three reasons for why they are:

> First, because the theologian considers human acts according as man is ordered to happiness through them. Now whatever is ordered to an end must be proportioned to the end. But acts are proportioned to the end according to a certain measure, which results from due circumstances. Hence, the theologian needs to consider circumstances. Second, because the theologian investigates human acts as good or evil, better and worse, and this diversity results from circumstances, as we shall show later on [q. 18, aa. 10–11; q. 73, a. 4]. Third, the theologian investigates human acts as having merit or demerit, which is proper to human acts; and for this it is necessary that acts be voluntary. Now human acts are judged to be voluntary or involuntary according to

> knowledge or ignorance of circumstances, as we have said [q. 6, a. 8]. Hence the theologian needs to consider circumstances. (Q. 7, a. 2)

This is not only a claim about the extent of the theologian's appropriate interests in regard to ethics, and thus peripheral to the main discussion about the rightness or wrongness of acts themselves, but also an account of what we need to consider in order to judge an act as right or wrong. Theology shares a concern for circumstances with moral philosophy, statecraft, and rhetoric, Thomas says. From the perspective of moral philosophy, circumstances determine the "mean of virtue," while from the point of view of statecraft and rhetoric circumstances have to do with whether an act should be rewarded or punished, praised or blamed (ibid.). Thomas is telling us here the direction that our questioning about the morality of acts needs to take. He is directing our attention to the acts themselves. If we want to know whether an act is right or wrong, virtuous or malicious, and deserving of praise or blame, we need to inquire into the circumstances of the act. From the perspective of moral philosophy, we need to know what the relevant circumstances are in order to determine whether an act is virtuous or not. From the perspective of the agent acting, what is needed is a set of virtues that will enable one to act appropriately with respect to circumstances.

Thomas's list of circumstances pertinent to a determination of whether or not an act is praiseworthy is adopted from Aristotle (*Nicomachean Ethics* III, 1). The relevant circumstances, according to the account Thomas adopts, are really a set of questions one asks about an act: "who, what, where, by what aids, why, how, and when" (q. 7, a. 3). The answers to questions about *who* did an act, *what* act was done, *where* was it done, and so forth, determine the act's moral species. In that respect, the two most important circumstances are *why* and *what is done*, the former because it specifies the end, which is the will's "object and motive," and the latter because it specifies the substance of the act. The end "is the most important cause of the act insofar as it moves the agent to act," Thomas explains (q. 7, a. 4). Once again, Thomas's discussion is oriented directly to an ethics of virtue. The list of circumstances surrounding acts is a kind of description of the terrain in which the cardinal virtues under the direction of prudence operate. Prudence and the other virtues enable someone to consider the circumstances and act well. Someone who acts according to virtue is someone who is well disposed to ends (described by the circumstance why), prompted by the right reasons and acting in the right way, right place, and at the right time. A virtuous person acts appropriately to his or her responsibilities on a particular occasion and in a particular situation. In other words, the virtues under the direction of prudence enable an individual to act in a manner befitting the circumstances. Whether or not this was the case on a specific occasion for moral judgment is what an inquiry into circumstances aims to discover.

III

So far, the procedure I have been following has been to investigate Thomas's most sustained treatment of ethics, the *Prima Secundae,* following his order of presentation, in order to determine whether an account of his ethics that stresses the virtue of prudence is a more adequate representation of what he says than the standard account's emphasis on natural law. I should acknowledge, at this point, that this question of mine is not necessarily an explicit question for Thomas. I am not at all trying to suggest that the tension or conflict between prudence and natural law occasioned by the history of interpretation of Thomas is a tension with which Thomas himself is directly concerned in his discussion. There may be grounds for arguing that this is one of Thomas's concerns because of his attempt to combine Aristotle with the existing theological tradition that employed a doctrine of natural law, but that is not the argument that I am trying to make.

The material I have discussed so far has been Thomas's introduction to ethics, an overview of what the moral analysis of human acts and character is about, that has not been primarily concerned with the specific virtue of prudence or with natural law. I have been arguing that there has been nothing in what Thomas has said to suggest his dependence on anything resembling the doctrine of natural law attributed to him. Although I have been saying that his discussion suggests the central importance of the virtues and especially prudence, there has not yet been an occasion where Thomas has stated as much explicitly. Much of my argument has been inferential and directed toward what Thomas will say when he discusses virtue specifically. In Thomas's analysis of the will in questions 8 through 18, however, the evidence becomes more substantial.

Thomas begins the discussion by returning to his claim that the will tends toward the good and to his earlier remark that the end to which the will tends is not necessarily a true good, but only apprehended as good (q. 8, a. 1). He goes on in the next question to state that it is the intellect's practical, as opposed to speculative, activity that moves the will by presenting an object to it as good (q. 9, a. 1). The particular relevance of this position for an ethics of virtue becomes explicit in Thomas's affirmation that there is a way in which the sense appetite moves the will:

> As we have said above [a. 1], that which is apprehended as being good and fitting is what moves the will as an object. Now something may seem to be good and fitting in two ways, either from the condition of the thing proposed *or of the one to whom it is proposed*. Since fittingness is based upon a relation, it depends upon each extreme of the relation. Thus taste, as it is differently disposed, reacts differently to what is fitting or unfitting. Hence the Philosopher says that "according as a man is, such does the end seem to him." [*Nicomachean Ethics* III, 5]
> *Now it is clear that a man is changed as to his disposition according to the passions of the sense appetite.* Hence something seems fitting to man when experiencing a certain passion which would not seem so with the passion absent; for example, something seems good to a man when angry which does not seem so when he is calm. In this way, on the part of the object, the sense appetite moves the will. (Q. 9, a. 2; emphasis added)

This is a straightforward statement about why our apprehension of particular ends as good is frequently mistaken. Whether something appears good depends not only on the thing itself but also on the disposition of the character of the one perceiving it. If one's character is corrupted, bad things appear good and good things seem bad. One's character is corrupt when the passions, which Thomas will describe in some detail, are not ordered by the virtues. Obviously, the companion to this portrayal of how the will is moved toward particular ends perceived as good is the account of the virtues and the passions that occupies subsequent questions of the *Prima Secundae.* Our apprehension of the good depends on our character, not on a set of natural attributes that form the foundation for a theory of natural law. In the concluding article of question 9, however, in which Thomas argues that God is the only extrinsic principle moving the will, there is a discussion of how the will is moved that is compatible with a doctrine of natural law properly understood.

The understanding of natural law that Thomas employs at this point functions to *explain* moral reasoning without providing epistemic grounds for making particular moral decisions. The reasons Thomas gives for why God is the extrinsic "cause of the will" are the familiar claims that God created the will as one of the rational soul's powers and that the will so created is "ordered to the universal good," which is none other than God himself (q. 9, a. 6). In other words, by virtue of their created nature humans will the good. But the good they can universally be said to will naturally is abstract in that it is the good in general. In reality, according to Thomas, the one ultimate human good is God, but not all are aware of that reality in the course of willing particular ends perceived as good. "God as the universal mover moves the will of man to the universal object of the will, which is the good," he says. "Without this universal motion, man cannot will anything. *But man by his reason determines himself to will this or that thing, which is either a true good or an apparent good"* (ibid., reply to objection 3; emphasis added). The law of our nature is necessarily to will the good. Every end we will is apprehended as good. We are limited, however, in that nothing in our nature guarantees that we apprehend goods correctly.

Thomas's remarks in question 10, article 1, concerning whether or not the will is naturally moved, make this suggestion about how to understand natural law even more plausible. His defense of the proposition that some things are willed naturally begins by pointing out different ways in which the word "nature" is used:

> Sometimes it is said of the intrinsic principle of things which move; in this sense, nature is the matter or form of the material thing. In another way, it is said of the substance or even of any being of the thing, and in this sense something is said to be natural to a thing which is proper to it according to its substance; this is what is essential to the thing. Now whatever is not essential to a thing is reducible to a principle that is essential to the thing. Hence, taking nature in this way, the principle of what belongs to a thing must always be a natural principle. This is clearly evident in the case of the intellect, for the principles of intellectual knowledge are naturally known. Similarly, the principle of voluntary movements must be something naturally willed.

> *Now this is the good in general, which the will naturally tends to as any power does to its object; it is also the ultimate end, which is related to all desirable things as the first principles of demonstration are to all intelligible things.* (Q. 10, a. 1; emphasis added)

Thomas's statement that we *naturally* will the good, seen in this light, does not commit him in the least to a doctrine with claims about our natural willing of specific goods. "Natural law" here has nothing to do with concrete moral knowledge but is rather the doctrine that humans are rational creatures created in such a way that the "law" or governing pattern of their nature is to tend toward the apprehended good in general. Whenever we will, however, we will something concrete. Because we are creatures with intellectual and sensitive powers directed by the will, our desire for the good is always pursued through what is apprehended as good for the intellect and the senses. Thus, "we do not seek through the will only what belongs to the power of the will, but also what belongs to each of the other powers and to man as a whole. Hence, man not only wills the object of the will [the good in general], but also whatever belongs to the other powers; for example, the knowledge of the truth, which belongs to the intellect; to exist and to live, and other things like this which concern his natural well-being. All of these are included under the object of the will as various particular goods" (q. 10, a. 1).

This statement should not be construed as a reference to the conception of natural law that I have been arguing that Thomas lacks. Its context is an explanation of what it means to say that what the will wills—the good in general—it wills naturally. The various powers under the direction of the will share in its orientation to the good. The intellect tends toward the good under the aspect of truth and the bodily powers tend toward the good under the aspect of sensible pleasures like the satisfaction of hunger. There is no suggestion that one can judge that a particular end is good in truth from the mere fact that one apprehends and wills it as good. Thomas has already argued quite the contrary position: Different individuals apprehend the goodness of various ends differently according to the virtuous or vicious nature of their dispositions.

The only thing that is necessarily willed by nature, Thomas reiterates, is the apprehended good in general, or in a more properly theological way of speaking, the ultimate end, "because it is the complete good." Even in saying that we necessarily will our complete good, however, Thomas is far from saying that we will fellowship with God, which is our complete good in reality. What we necessarily will is the good, but only the good in general, whatever it is that we take to be our good within the limits of our apprehension.

He includes as part of what necessarily moves the will "whatever else is ordered to such an end without which the end cannot be attained, such as to exist and to live, and things of this kind" (q. 10, a. 2; reply to objection 3). It is important to note that the question at issue in article 2 is whether "the will is necessarily moved by its object," and that Thomas is defending the freedom of the will. The specific objection to which he is responding states that the will must be moved by various objects other than the end in question because in willing any end we also necessarily will the means. Thomas grants that the will is necessarily moved to the good in general, or to the ultimate end, and to the necessary conditions of the possibility of achieving the end, such as remaining alive, but he immediately adds that "*other things, without which the end can be had, are not willed necessarily by one who wills the end,* just as one who assents to the principles does not necessarily assent to the conclusions, without which the principles can be true" (ibid.; emphasis added).

One reason it seems implausible to try to derive much concrete guidance for moral decision making from human nature, on the basis of what Thomas has said, is that according to Thomas, God created our nature to be indeterminately ordered to any specific ends. He can say, therefore, that the will is not even moved with necessity by God, because God only moves things "in accordance with their condition," and the nature of the human condition is open, or indeterminately oriented to any specific good. "The will," he insists, "is an active principle which is not determined to one thing, but is related indifferently to many." When God moves it, "He does not determine it to one thing with necessity, but leaves its movement contingent and not necessary, except in regard to which it is moved naturally" (q. 10, a. 4). And we have already seen that what the will is moved to naturally is only the last end, the ultimate good, or from the perspective of this world, the good in general insofar as every particular end that we will we apprehend as good.

Thomas's perspective, therefore, leaves very little room for a full-fledged ethics of natural law. The foundations required by such a theory seem to have been drastically undermined by Thomas's portrayal of a human nature created in such a way that it is oriented by nature only to its final end and is unavoidably free to direct itself to more particular ends. (Of course, we always find ourselves already willing particular goods. Thomas is not saying that we are free to refrain from all such willing of ends or that we can do our willing in a vacuum void of previous attachments.) Human nature, according to Thomas's analysis, provides no concrete moral guidance. The "law" of our nature seems to be that we act on the basis of apprehended goods, although (whether or not we know it on the basis of revelation) we are created in such a way as to be ordered to God. That very description of human nature positively invites an ethics of virtue because our apprehension of appropriate goods is a matter of the disposition of our character.

The virtues do not operate autonomously but are coordinated and directed by reason through the virtue of prudence. The significance of prudence begins to become apparent in Thomas's treatment of the various acts of the will, especially his treatment of choice, an act of the will directed by prudence. Thomas begins by establishing that choice, like the acts of enjoyment and intention, is basically an appetitive rather than intellectual act (q. 13, aa. 1–3). Choice is the act of the will concerned with means toward ends and does not belong to irrational creatures because they are naturally determined to certain "choices" through their sense appetite. Humans, in contrast, are not naturally determined but are free to choose for themselves. The human will, Thomas observes, "though determined by nature to something one in general, the good, is undetermined with respect to particular goods" (q. 13, a. 2).

Thomas's initial statement that choice, properly speaking, has to do with means rather than ends would seem to limit the claims that could be made for the overall importance of prudence in moral deliberation: "[C]hoice follows upon a decision or a judgment, which is like the conclusion of an operative [practical] syllogism. Hence what the operative syllogism concludes to falls under choice. Now in the practical order, the end is like a principle, not a conclusion, as Aristotle remarks [*Nicomachean Ethics* IV, 12]. Therefore, the end as such is not a matter of choice" (q. 13, a. 3). If this were all Thomas said, this passage might be taken as evidence for the standard interpretation of Thomas's teaching, that we have a natural knowledge of moral principles specific enough to serve as the premises of practical syllogisms. Because premises or principles in the practical order are like ends and not a matter of choice, it would seem that the deliberations enabled by the virtue of prudence have to do only with conclusions, the means toward ends. This would seem to refute my claim that the standard version of natural law misrepresents Thomas's position by limiting prudence's activity to deliberation about means to ends that are naturally known through the insights of synderesis.

Immediately, however, Thomas moves in a different direction. He says in the very next paragraph that "just as in the speculative order nothing prevents the principle of one demonstration or of one science from being the conclusion of another demonstration or science—though a first indemonstrable principle cannot be the conclusion of any demonstration or science—so also what is the end of one action can be ordered to something else as an end. In this way, the end can be a matter of choice" (q. 13, a. 3). Thomas is saying here that in the realm of action every end can also be viewed as the means to another end, which is entirely consistent with his repeated claim that there is only one ultimate end to which every other end is subordinated. In that case choice, and therefore prudence, can be referred to ends as well as means. In fact, it is more accurate to say that from Thomas's perspective, according to which human acts are considered ultimately in terms of their orientation to the final end of our proper happiness, every act is a means to that end and thus a legitimate object of choice and a concern of prudence. It is not only with respect to our ultimate end that other ends are describable as means; Thomas says the same thing about the relation between subsidiary ends. For example, in his subsequent discussion of the passions of hatred and love he notes that the end of avoiding an evil is actually a means directed toward obtaining some good (q. 29, a. 3).

If this interpretation sounds fanciful, consider Thomas's replies to the two objections in question 13, article 3, which state that "choice is about the end" (objection 1) or at least "about ends as well as means" (objection 2). Thomas's answer is an instance where he elaborates on the objections, rather than refuting them, in order to make clear the sense in which they are correct: He says in his reply to objection 1, "The proper ends of the virtues are ordered to happiness as to the ultimate end. In this way ends can be a matter of choice." His answer to objection 2 is to reiterate that "there is only one ultimate end. Hence, when there are a number of ends there can be choice among them inasmuch as they are ordered to an ultimate end" (ibid.).

Thomas's reply to the question of whether an individual chooses with necessity or not (q. 13, a. 6) restates the previous article's contention that although choice, *per se,* is about means and not ends, one can freely choose any specific and subordinate end. Although happiness is necessarily willed, he reminds the reader, the will can tend to the infinite variety of ends rightly or wrongly apprehended by reason as good and conducive to happiness. We can be said to choose freely because "choice, since it is not about the end but the means, . . . is not about the perfect good which is happiness, but about particular goods" (q. 13, a. 6).

This is a rich statement that casts considerable light on Thomas's understanding of our orientation to the good and of the function of prudence. Strictly speaking, choice is about means and not about ends. Because every act can be considered as an end, however, and because every end can be considered as a means to the ultimate end, choice is also about ends. The only end to which our will is necessarily oriented by nature is the apprehended good in general or the complete good, our ultimate end. We are inescapably free to choose subordinate ends or specific goods. This does not mean, however, that we deliberate about the selection of each good to which we are oriented or that we make choices apart from the influence of attachments to other goods. Indeed, we find ourselves, on reflection, oriented to a variety of goods we did not consciously choose. The point is that our attachments to any particular goods could conceivably always be otherwise than they are. We are not necessitated to particular goods by nature. Because the will's act of choice requires perfection by a virtue, which turns out to be the virtue of prudence, prudence is necessarily concerned with the ends of action, which are the means to our ultimate end. In other words, subordinate goods are something about which we are able to choose because we are only necessitated to the ultimate good. In order to choose, we have to deliberate, and in order to deliberate and choose well we need the virtue of prudence. Willing the right good and choosing the right means both require prudence.

Our apprehension of the goodness of particular ends is free from determination by necessity, Thomas insists in response to an objection. Objection 2 (q. 13, a. 6) states, as a premise to the conclusion that choice is necessitated, that choice chooses as reason judges, and that reason reaches necessary judgments when its principles are necessary. Thomas's reply underlines his view of moral decision making as a realm of rational judgment in which the certainty of the standard versions of natural law is out of place. "Reason's decision or judgment of what is to be done is about contingent matters which can be done by us. In these matters, conclusions do not necessarily follow from necessary principles with absolute necessity, but only conditionally" (q. 13, a. 6; reply to objection 2).

Thomas again emphasizes, at the beginning of the next question, the uncertainty and contingency that characterize the sphere of human action with which moral deliberation is concerned. Once again, his remarks underscore the importance of prudence. The first article in question 14 concerns whether or not the activity of deliberation preceding choice should be characterized as an inquiry. Thomas says that moral questions about human actions are fraught with uncertainty because actions are singular and contingent things and therefore variable. We are not in the realm of universal and necessary truths. It is unreasonable, he says, to choose what is to be done in any situation without inquiring about its particularities. "[T]his inquiry is called taking counsel or deliberating" (q. 14, a. 1), and is characteristic of the prudent individual, someone who deliberates well.

The direction of the deliberation or inquiry is toward the concrete particularity of the situation in question, the focus of prudence. In Thomas's subsequent discussion of prudence it becomes evident that prudence shares attributes of the intellectual as well as the moral virtues. (The role of prudence in Aristotle's account of moral deliberation and decision making, upon which Thomas draws extensively, as well as the various attributes of prudence, is carefully explored by Troels Engberg-Pedersen, 1983. See also H. H. Joachim's commentary on *The Nicomachean Ethics*, 1951.) Thomas's remarks here about deliberation provide some suggestions about why that should be the case and about why the standard account's sharp distinction between knowledge of ends, the realm of natural law, and deliberation about means, the concern of prudence, is misleading. The rational activity of deliberation and the consequent appetitive activity of choice are so interrelated in practice that the theoretical distinctions between the powers concerned with ends and means once again become blurred. Prudence, the virtue pertaining to rational deliberation about things that we will, is necessarily oriented to both our deliberative and appetitive capacities, the intellect and the will:

> When the acts of two powers are ordered to one another, there is something in each belonging to the other power, and hence each act can be denominated from either power. Now it is clear that an act of reason directing in regard to the means, and an act of the will tending to the means according to reason's direction, are ordered to one another. Hence in choice, an act of the will, there is something of reason, namely, order; and in deliberation, an act of reason, there is something of the will, as matter, for delibera-

tion concerns what man wishes to do, and also as mover, for from the fact that man wills an end he is moved to deliberate about the means. Hence the Philosopher says that "choice is reason influenced by desire" [*Nicomachean Ethics* VI. 2], thereby indicating that both concur in the act of choice." (Q. 14, a. 1)

This is why Thomas later describes the relation between prudence and the other cardinal virtues as one of reciprocity and why he insists that one cannot be prudent in the absence of fortitude, temperance, and justice or why one cannot be virtuous without being prudent. Prudence is the rational activity of deliberation, preceding choice, which coordinates and directs the activity of the other virtues. The other virtues, in turn, determine our apprehension of the goods about which we wish to deliberate.

The next article raises the specific question of whether deliberation is about ends or means. One might think that since the article begins by stating *it would seem* that deliberation is about ends as well as means, that Thomas would reply in the negative. His discussion of deliberation, however, parallels the discussion of choice. He begins by again drawing the analogy between the ends in actions and basic principles in speculative inquiries: Just as basic principles must be presupposed, ends also are beyond the scope of deliberation, which has to do with means. Thomas goes on, however, once again to make the point that the end of one action can be the means to another end, and in that sense subject to deliberation (q. 14, a. 2). The natural lawyer's relegation of prudence to a deliberation only about means fails to reflect this complexity.

Article three of the same question is particularly suggestive about the pragmatic importance of prudence's orientation to the specifics of circumstances and about the relative insignificance, for practical purposes, of speculative truths. In affirming the proposition that deliberation and the taking of counsel concern things that we do, Thomas describes moral judgment by contrasting it to speculative reasoning. He once again mentions the singularity, contingency, and variety of circumstances impinging on human action and observes that by the very nature of its object moral deliberation is made more certain when several individuals deliberate together, "for what one notices escapes the attention of another" (q. 14, a. 3). In contrast, no such consultative inquiry is needed "in necessary and universal matters." Truth in contingent things is less intrinsically desirable, he adds, "but it is desirable as useful for action, for actions concern singular contingent events" (ibid.).

Truth in matters of moral choice, it appears, is not reached intuitively. Moral knowledge requires familiarity with details of the situations that prompt questions of moral choice. It depends on the cumulative and shared experience of people conversing with each other rather than on the insights of solitary introspection. The kind of reasoning to which Thomas is referring is a skill that requires cultivation rather than an innate possession. According to natural-law theory, in contrast, one has a natural knowledge of a variety of ends — more or less extensive depending on the particular version of the theory — and then reasons, with the aid of the virtue of prudence, about means. According to what Thomas says here, quite the opposite is true: One is naturally inclined to the good in general or to the ultimate end, to which every other end can be viewed as a means. Although the various powers of reason and appetite, which are properly under the direction of prudence and the other virtues, are in one sense concerned with means, Thomas repeatedly points out the moral sense in which they refer to ends.

Another good example of this tendency occurs in Thomas's remarks about the will's activity of consenting, which follows deliberation. What desire tends to naturally is the ultimate end, Thomas says, and "properly speaking," deliberation and consent have to do with means. He immediately adds, however, that "the things we direct our attention to after the ultimate end, in so far as they are for the end, fall under deliberation, and so there can be consent about them inasmuch as the appetitive movement is applied to what has been decided upon by deliberation" (q. 15, a. 4).

The lesson to be drawn from this is that the moral terrain under the purview of the virtues extends up to our created tendency to the ultimate end, which is where Thomas talks about natural inclination. So far, Thomas has declined to use the vocabulary of natural inclination for subordinate ends. Those subordinate ends can be described as means to the ultimate end and thus can be seen as the objects of the intellectual and appetitive powers concerned with means, but we are only indeterminately ordered to all of them. (The only exception is Thomas's remark, noted above, that we can be said to be inclined naturally to those things necessary for tending toward the good at all. The only example he gives of that exception is a general inclination to "existence," and he later adds an interesting qualification. "Properly speaking," he observes, "it is impossible for a man to hate himself." Addressing the example of apparent self-hate in the case of suicides, however, he notes that "they who kill themselves, apprehend death itself as a good, considered as putting an end to unhappiness or pain" (q. 29, a. 4). Even in the case of life itself, therefore, we still are oriented only to the good in general or to the apparent good. We do not automatically, universally, or necessarily will even the most seemingly fundamental good of existence. Sometimes, death is apprehended as a good.)

Thomas is slightly more specific in article 4 of question 16 about what he means when he talks about the will's natural tendency. He says that the will tends to something in two ways. The first way has to do with "the willed thing's being in some way in the one who wills through some proportion or order to that willed thing. Hence things that are naturally proportioned to some end are said to desire it naturally" (q. 16, a. 4). This provides little support for an elaborate theory of natural law, however, because so far the only thing Thomas has said that we are naturally ordered or proportioned to is happiness or the good in general (and the most general conditions for its pursuit), which he holds to be only finally achievable through ultimate union with God. He goes on to say in the same article that to have an end in the sense of being naturally ordered to it is to have it imperfectly (ibid.). The second way the will is related to an end is to have it really, or perfectly, which involves willing not only the end, but also the means (ibid.), and which is the context where the vocabulary of virtue, rather than natural law, is appropriate.

Although a thorough discussion of Thomas's treatment of the morality of human acts is beyond the scope of this study, it will be useful to survey the final section of the "Treatise on Happiness" for more evidence about the relative importance of prudence or natural law. If Thomas were expounding the theory of natural law ordinarily attributed to him, one would expect him to make use of the theory in his discussion of how human acts in general can be judged as good or evil (q. 18). Instead, he relies on the vocabulary of virtue, as he did in the preceding analysis of the will. First of all, he says that acts are good to the extent that they are in accord with right reason. A natural-law theorist would be quite happy with the formulation that goodness of acts is to be determined by right reason, assuming that right reason refers to an innate capacity of human nature or to some logical requirement about the conclusions of practical delib-eration imposed by the very nature of reason. Thomas, however, does not say anything like that in this section. Instead, he says quite plainly that reason is right to the extent that it is in accord with virtue.

He begins the discussion by equating the goodness of any thing with its fullness of being and its maliciousness with its lack of being. There is a degree of goodness in any act insofar as it merely exists. What it means for a human act to lack being, he explains, is to lack "the quantity determined by reason, or due place, or something of this kind" (q. 18, a. 1). This should sound familiar because it is a reference to the importance of circumstances. In the context of this discussion, as in the previous discussion of circumstances, Thomas is referring to reason's practical concern with the contingent factors surrounding an act that help us identify the act as good or evil. What it means for a human act to lack fullness of being is not for it to lack correspondence to some description of the universal and changeless features of human nature, but to lack fittingness to the particular and temporary features of the situation in which the act occurs, which is a determination made accurately by an individual with practical experience, or prudence.

The second factor influencing the goodness or evil of an action is "the appropriateness [or inappropriateness] of its object" (q. 18, a. 2), the thing that we will (hitting a man, for example), which places the act in its species or determines what kind of an act it is. Although Thomas does not say so immediately, it soon becomes apparent that the appropriateness of an object of an act is determined with reference to reason made right by virtue. Third, an act receives further moral definition from its circumstances (already enumerated in question 7: who, what or about what, where, by what aids, why, how, and when). In defense of the proposition that circumstances do in fact make an act good or bad, Thomas quotes Aristotle's claim (*Nicomachean Ethics* II, 3) "that a virtuous man acts as he should act, when he should, and so on according to other circumstances" (q. 18, a. 3). Finally, an act is good or evil depending on what its end is (q. 18, a. 4), that is, what it is that we hope to accomplish through the act (hitting a man with the end of saving the lives of innocent victims he is attacking). Thomas goes on to note that an act has to be good in all four of these interrelated ways in order to be good absolutely. It is vitiated by a defect in any one of the ways:

> Hence a fourfold goodness can be considered in human action. The first is the goodness an action has in terms of its genus, namely, as an action, for it has as much of goodness as it has of action and being, as we have said. Second, an action has goodness according to its species, which it has from its appropriate object. Third, it has goodness from its circumstances — its accidents,

as it were. Fourth, it has goodness from its end, which is related to
it as a cause of its goodness. (Ibid.)

Thomas's presumption of a theory of virtue in this discussion becomes
apparent in the next article, where he insists that good and evil acts
constitute two different species. His initial refutation of the contrary
position (that good and evil acts are the same species) is an argument
from the observation that good habits are of a different species than evil
habits, and that acts resulting from particular habits are like them in
species (q. 18, a. 5). Good and evil habits, of course, are none other than
virtues and vices. His developed argument that good and evil acts differ in
species proceeds from the premise that "human acts are called good or
evil in relation to reason" because the human good is constituted by a life
in accord with reason (ibid.). (Remember his previous, and equivalent,
formulation that the human good is a life in accordance with virtue.) He
then notes that this difference in good or evil, with respect to the object of
an act, is a *per se* difference, constituting a difference in species (ibid.).
The argument itself may fail to impress or even make sense to modern
readers, but what is important is the identification of human reason as the
referent for the goodness of human acts. Thomas calls reason the "principle"
of human acts and argues that they are good, evil, or morally indifferent
to the extent that they are in harmony with, opposed to, or indifferent to
reason (q. 18, a. 8). He says that if an act "is ordered to a due end, it is in
conformity with the order of reason, and so is counted as good," assuming
that it is not vitiated by inappropriate circumstances (q. 18, a. 9).

To find support for a theory of natural law here one has to equate
Thomas's reference to right reason with some natural ordering of reason
to specific ends so far unspecified by Thomas. What Thomas does say
specifically, instead, is that right reason about action is related to virtue:
"Every end intended by deliberative reason pertains to the good of some
virtue or to the evil of some vice" (q. 18, a. 9). To act in accord with
reason is to act in accord with virtue, and *vice versa*. To act thus is
certainly to act in accord with nature, but to say this is not to add
additional information. The good of our nature is precisely virtuous and
rational activity.

Moreover, he contrasts rather than compares the natural species of
things and the moral species of acts: A thing's natural species is determined by its natural form, while an act's moral species depends on an
act's form "as conceived by reason" (q. 18, a. 10). Although there is

an ultimate natural form for every thing, determining its species with
finality, the moral species of acts can vary indefinitely, depending on the
infinite variety of circumstances that conceivably can impinge on an act.
That is to say, one can always tell a story about an act in which its moral
species changes from good to evil, as the result of a specific circumstance that is a "principle condition" of the act's object. The natural
species of things are determined once and for all, but the moral species
of acts can vary as their circumstances vary. Thomas says that "the
process of reason is not determined to something one, for with whatever
is given, it can still proceed further. Accordingly, what is taken in a given
act as a circumstance added to the object which specifies the act, can be
taken by reason's power of ordering things, as a principle condition of the
object determining the species of an act" (ibid.). For example, having
sexual intercourse with one's spouse is ordinarily a good act. But if the
circumstance "where" happens to be "on the altar in church," that
circumstance, in the absence of an extraordinarily improbable countervailing
principle condition, renders the deed an evil act of profaning a sacred
place.

This is not at all to say that the rightness or wrongness of an act already
identified in a moral species is somehow ambiguous. Profaning a sacred
place, withholding the truth from whom it is due, and causing pain to
others for fun are acts that are absolutely wrong and contrary to the virtue
of justice at the very least. Thomas is not saying that in some circumstances morally vicious acts are somehow made acceptable. Rather, he is
saying that the initial moral identification of any human act is determined
with reference to the four criteria of reason, object, circumstance, and
end, which themselves are referred to reason rectified by virtue or, which
is the same thing, to virtue directed by reason.

The act of raising one's hand can have immensely different moral
meanings in different circumstances. It might be a virtuous act of
volunteering the truth, a vicious act of giving a signal for the murder of an
innocent victim, or an indifferent act of stretching. Because of the infinite
variety of ends that reason can choose, and because of the variety of
circumstances surrounding every act, the process of moral identification
is never over. The tendency of natural-law theories, however, is to obscure
this complexity by making the identification of moral species equivalent
to the identification of natural species, quite contrary to what Thomas
argues throughout this section.

After concluding the discussion of how human acts in general are to be judged as good or evil, Thomas turns to the question of how to judge the goodness or maliciousness of the interior act of the will. Once more, everything hinges on right reason in accord with virtue. In the first article of question 19, arguing that the act of the will is good with reference to its object, Thomas describes a good will as "one that is in accord with virtue" and therefore wills a good object. In the replies to objections he reminds readers that the will tends to what reason presents to it as an apparent good. When the object of the will accords with right reason, "it corresponds to what is moral and causes moral goodness in the act of the will" (q. 19, a. 1).

Question 19 is especially significant for this study and warrants detailed discussion because it addresses the issue of the relation between the goodness of the will and human knowledge of eternal law directly and refers to prudence explicitly. Article 1 concludes by stressing reason as "the principle of human and moral acts" (reply to objection 3), and article 3 addresses the question of the will's dependence on reason for its goodness. According to the objections in the article, the goodness of the will depends first and foremost on the will itself because the will appre-hends something as good before reason does and because the will moves reason. Objection 2 quotes Aristotle's claim that "the goodness of the practical intellect is truth in conformity with right desire" (*Nicomachean Ethics* VI, 2), equates right desire with a good will, and concludes that "the goodness of practical reason depends more upon the goodness of the will rather than the converse" (q. 19, a. 3). "On the contrary," Thomas says, "the goodness of the will depends upon its being subject to reason" (ibid.). He explains in his general response that the will's goodness depends on its choice of an object, which is initially presented by reason.

Thomas's specific reply to objection 2 illustrates his understanding of prudence's orientation to reason as well as to will, its reciprocal relation with other virtues, and the extent to which virtue is his predominate theme: He says that Aristotle's statement that the practical intellect's goodness is a matter of right desire concerns prudence's activity of determining right means. Right reason about means, the specific concern of prudence, requires the willing of an appropriate end, however, which as he has already suggested is the concern of the moral virtues. A right will, in turn, requires that the end be rightly understood, "and this is the work of reason" (q. 19, a. 3). But this work of reason also pertains to prudence because, as we have seen, every end of an action can also be viewed as a means to the ultimate end.

If the goodness of the will depends on reason, the next article suggests, then it would seem that the eternal law is irrelevant (q. 19, a. 4). Thomas's reply that the will's goodness does in fact depend on eternal law might seem at first to be his vehicle for belatedly introducing natural law. A closer examination of this article and the two that immediately follow it, however, shows that what might be interpreted as natural-law language serves an explanatory rather than an epistemic function, and that questions about moral knowledge depend on the view of practical reason oriented to prudence.

The entirety of question 19 concerns the goodness of the will, and the specific issue in article 4 is whether *the will,* not an act of another power, depends on the *eternal law,* not the natural law, for its goodness. Thomas affirms that the goodness of the will does indeed depend on eternal law, which is not a legal code but rather God's overarching wisdom and plan for creation, and his explanation focuses on causality. He says that the eternal law is the cause for "human reason's capacity to be the rule of human will, by which its goodness is measured" (q. 19, a. 4). He quotes Psalms 4:7, "The light of Thy countenance, O Lord, is signed upon us," in support of the claim that the will's goodness ultimately *depends* on the eternal law of God who created human reason with the ability to distinguish good from evil and to regulate the will. Finally, he introduces the claim that "when human reason fails, we must have recourse to eternal reason" (ibid.), which is revealed in scripture and in which we share insofar as we act for a good.

According to Christian natural-law theory, we have a natural knowledge of at least part of the *content* of God's eternal moral law, but that is not what Thomas is saying here. Our knowledge of eternal law is different from God's, Thomas says. Although he observes that "it is known by us *in a certain way,* either through natural reason, which is derived from the divine mind as a proper image of it, or by some kind of revelation which is added over and beyond" (ibid.; reply to objection 3), there is nothing in this statement as it stands that warrants the standard natural-law reading of Thomas's ethics. Instead, the observation about human reason's mode of knowing the eternal law seems to be another expression of Thomas's previous claim about our orientation to the good and about the difference between our knowledge of the good and God's. God knows the proper good and end of things in reality while our apprehension of goodness, especially as it relates to specific ends of human action, is often mistaken. The way in which our practical reason is a reflection of the divine mind is in our created tendency to desire ends perceived as good and to be ordered to the good in general or to the ultimate good. (Thomas says this explicitly in article 10.) Thomas's statement here concerns natural law only in the sense that it is the "law" of our nature to act for ends apprehended, often mistakenly, as good. God also acts for the good, and in that respect our practical reason is a reflection of divine reason.

The plausibility of this interpretation is reinforced by Thomas's claim in article 5 that even an erring conscience binds us to act in accord with its judgment. He describes conscience as a "kind of dictate of reason" and a "certain kind of application of knowledge to act" and says that "a will at variance with erring reason is evil" (q. 19, a. 5). Thomas notes that some of those who distinguish acts as being good, evil, or indifferent "by nature" hold that conscience errs when it commands actually evil acts and forbids actually good acts. Conscience also errs, according to the view Thomas is describing in order to refute it, when conscience forbids or commands indifferent acts. Those who hold this view claim that the erring conscience only binds with respect to indifferent matters. They say that when conscience commands an actually evil act or forbids an actually good act, however, it does not bind. They conclude that in these cases, the will that refuses the command of an erring conscience is not evil (q. 19, a. 5).

Thomas rejects this entire position as unreasonable. The will at odds with an erring conscience is malicious with respect to the evil of the will's object, he explains, "*not because of the object according to its own nature*, but according as the object *is accidentally apprehended by reason* as something evil to do or to avoid" (ibid.; emphasis added). God knows the actual goodness of the will's objects, but we are obliged to act in accord with our apprehension of goodness even when our reason or conscience is in error. Thomas states without equivocation that "from the fact that something is proposed by reason as evil, the will, by tending to it is evil," not only when the end in question is indifferent, but also when the end is actually good or evil. The reason, he says, is that "what is good can take on the character of evil, and what is evil that of good, because of reason grasping something in this way" (ibid.). His two striking examples leave his position beyond a doubt: If reason judges that refraining from fornication is evil, then the will that disobeys that judgment and refrains is also evil. Likewise, if reason proposes faith in Christ as evil, the will that tends toward faith is evil. In short, "every will that is at variance with reason, whether right or wrong, is always evil" (ibid.).

The significance of this article for our purposes lies in Thomas's insistence on referring moral judgment to fallible and uncertain human reason, requiring the direction of virtue, rather than to some supposedly invariable and certain standard in nature. What is certain, according to Thomas, is God's knowledge and our obligation to act in accord with virtue and right reason. He does not say that we can look to an abstract conception of human nature, or to the nature of human reason, for specific moral information. Although our reason reflects something of the divine mind, according to Thomas, our knowledge of God's will is radically limited. All that we know is that "whatever God wills, he wills it under the aspect of good" (q. 19, a. 10).

It sometimes happens that our apprehension of good and God's certain knowledge of good coincide, so Thomas can say that "whoever wills something inasmuch as it is good has his will conformed to the divine will with respect to the nature of what is willed" (ibid.), but apart from revelation we have no concrete source of information about the content of God's will. Because "we do not know what God wills in particular, in this respect we are not bound to conform our will to the divine will" (ibid.). Only in the next life will everyone "see in each thing that he wills the order that thing has to what God wills" (ibid.). In this life, reason has to be made right by virtue. As Thomas says in the very next question, "right reasoning in accordance with end of the virtues has no other goodness than the goodness of virtue, inasmuch as any virtue participates in the goodness of reason" (q. 20, a. 3; reply to objection 2). The virtue he mentions in particular as pertaining to right reason about action is prudence, "which is in reason, [and] is ordered to things that are for an end" (ibid.).

Nowhere in the "Treatise on Happiness," the first section of the *Prima Secundae,* does Thomas draw on anything like the theory of natural law ordinarily attributed to him. The treatise concludes with a discussion of the implications of an act being good or evil: its sinfulness or rightness, its praise- or blameworthiness. Here Thomas explicitly contrasts the measurement of a thing by nature and by reason, and associates the measurement of an act by reason with virtue. With respect to things whose actions are determined by nature, the rule of measurement "is the power of nature itself which inclines to a given end" (q. 20, a. 1). The example he gives is an act prompted by a natural power. In contrast, "in voluntary actions the proximate rule is human reason and the supreme rule is eternal law," and it is by those measures that actions are judged to be good or evil (ibid.). Thomas does not mention any intermediate epistemic standard of natural law. The sed contra of article 2, defending the claim that acts deserve praise or blame according as they are good or evil, straightforwardly equates reason's judgment about the good or evil of acts with virtue. "[G]ood acts are acts of virtue," he says, while "acts opposed to virtue are evil." And as Thomas notes in the same article, the moral virtues are under the direction of prudence (q. 20, a. 2; reply to objection 2).

IV

After concluding his analysis of human acts and the will and of the way in which they can be judged as good or evil, Thomas next proceeds to a long discussion (qq. 22–48) of the passions, or what we would call the emotions, the last topic he considers in his elaboration of the context for the virtues. Passions have to do with the interaction of the soul and various objects apprehended as good or evil. That is, they describe or name the mode in which the soul moves to or from an object acting upon it. Thomas locates the passions in the concupiscible and irascible powers of the sensitive appetite, each of which has its own set of passions, grouped (with one exception) in pairs of opposites. The concupiscible passions are "love and hatred, desire and aversion, joy and sadness," while the irascible passions are "hope and despair, fear and daring, and anger, which has no contrary" (q. 23, a. 4). Those associated with the concupiscible power concern "sensible good or evil, simply apprehended as such, which causes pleasure or pain . . . whereas those passions which regard good or bad as arduous, through being difficult to obtain or avoid, belong to the irascible faculty" (q. 23, a. 1). In themselves, Thomas says, the passions are morally neutral, a departure from the classical Stoic perspective, which viewed passions negatively. Regarded as under the control of the rational appetite, however, they concern virtues or vices: "[I]n so far as they are contrary to the order of reason," the passions "incline us to sin: but in so far as they are controlled by reason, they pertain to virtue" (q. 24, a. 2).

Thomas sees us as "passionate" creatures by nature, but our nature is such that our passions do not automatically correspond to the order of reason. They require ordering by the virtues under the direction of prudence. Thomas's discussion, in many ways, is an extension of what he has already said about the will's orientation to the good in general and its specific tendency to particular apprehended goods. It also anticipates the subsequent discussion of virtue and introduces the notion of natural inclinations, upon which so much natural-law speculation depends. Thomas's use of the adjective "natural" is hardly unambiguous, but its use here in connection with a discussion of tendencies to particular ends illustrates problems inherent in trying to derive concrete moral guidance from the notion.

He notes in his discussion of the passion of love, the source of all the other passions, that it "differs according to the difference of appetites" (q. 26, a. 1). There is a *natural* appetite of love, which has to do with something's created tendency to a particular end. Thomas says that this appetite follows from an apprehension existing in the creator rather than the creature. In the case of humans, as we already have seen, our natural appetite or love for the good in general is a manifestation of our created tendency to achieve the ultimate good only in union with God. There is also a *sensitive* appetite of love, shared by irrational animals and humans, which has to do with the subject's appetite following its own apprehension of something as good. The animal appetite for food would be an example. In animals, this operates from necessity, Thomas says, while in humans, in contrast, it "has a certain share of liberty, in so far as it obeys reason" (ibid.). Finally, "there is another appetite following freely from an apprehension in the subject of the appetite. And this is the rational or intellectual appetite, which is called the will" (ibid.). Thomas, as we have seen, repeatedly stresses the freedom and indeterminacy of this appetite which, like the human sensitive appetite in so far as it is subject to reason, is to be judged as good or evil according to its conformity to right reason.

The standard version of natural law requires some natural pattern of love, some natural tendency or inclination to a set of authentically good ends, to function normatively. The difficulty, however, is that Thomas's statements about our tendency, inclination, appetite, willing, or love of the good are regularly qualified by the observation that such a good is an *apparent* good. Whether or not actual goods appear good to us depends on right reason and virtue. How is one to judge whether reason is right or not? So far, Thomas has not said anything to suggest that the judgment is made by referring reason to the law of nature. In fact, this description of the hierarchy of appetites or inclinations of human nature in which our natural love is for the ultimate good and in which our animal and rational appetites are characterized by liberty, plus his insistence that the morally significant sphere of human action is that which is voluntary, appears to leave little room for a version of natural law dependent on a determinate set of normative inclinations.

In his affirmative response to the question of whether an agent does everything because of love, for example, he says: "Every agent acts for an end. . . . Now the end is the good desired and loved by each one. Wherefore it is evident that every agent, whatever it be, does every action from love of some kind" (q. 28, a. 6). If it were to turn out that we naturally love some goods that are good in reality and not merely apparent goods, those loves could be construed as normative. After all, Thomas says that as far as the natural appetite is concerned, there is a natural love of what is suitable to a subject and a natural hatred of what is destructive (q. 29, a. 1). In the case of rational creatures ordered by their creator to the ultimate good of union with God, however, the practical import of this is that we always act for the sake of an apparent good and never for the sake of an apparent evil, a claim that describes human action and explains it with reference to God's plan for creation, but which does not provide guidance for behavior.

Neither does Thomas's description of the animal appetite appear to provide a foundation for natural law. Granted, he says that for the animal appetite "love is a certain harmony . . . with that which is apprehended as suitable; while hatred is dissonance . . . for that which is apprehended as repugnant and hurtful," and that "whatever is suitable, as such, bears the aspect of good; so whatever is repugnant, as such, bears the aspect of evil" (q. 29, a. 1). But he also says that a *rational* animal's appetite is distinguished by its freedom. The general topic of question 29 is love's opposing passion of hatred, and in the first article Thomas argues that just as one is attracted to an apparent good, one is also repelled by an apparent evil. The emphasis is on "apparent": "Just as a thing may be apprehended as good, when it is not truly good; so a thing may be apprehended as evil, whereas it is not truly evil" (ibid.; reply to objection 2). He adds that the same object may be loved or hated by different subjects "owing to one and the same thing being apprehended by one as good, by another as bad" (ibid.; reply to objection 3).

In response to the question of whether concupiscences are appropriately divided into natural and unnatural desires, Thomas does recognize certain "natural" concupiscences, the desires for "food, drink, and the like" that "are common to men and other animals" and about which "all men agree" (q. 30, a. 3). He is arguing, however, against two opposing extreme views: first, that there are no natural concupiscences (objection 1) and second, that there are none that are not natural (objection 3). Against the first view he is merely making the claim that humans are not disembodied souls; they have an animal physiology with a "natural" desire for nourishment. Against the second view he argues that the existence of "unnatural" or rational desires beyond these is also characteristic of humans, "to whom it is proper to devise something as good and suitable, beyond that which nature requires," and about which "different men reason differently" (q. 30, a. 1; sed contra). It is primarily with these desires that moral investigation is concerned.

In the entire *Prima Secundae*, the first appearance of anything remotely like a natural-law argument occurs in a sentence in article 7 of question 31, which considers the passion of delight or pleasure. The issue in article 7 is whether or not some pleasures are unnatural. Thomas's argument that some pleasures are not natural, and his examples in support of that argument, might appear to count as evidence against my claim about the insignificance of natural law. He notes that "from custom some take pleasure in cannibalism or in the unnatural intercourse of man and beast, or other such like things, which are not in accord with human nature" (q. 31, a. 7). This might seem to be a straightforward natural-law judgment about the immorality of these practices. On a more careful reading, however, that is not what Thomas is saying.

It is important to remember that Thomas's specific discussion of whether some pleasures are not natural is part of a general discussion of the passion of delight or pleasure, which in turn is part of a larger treatment of all the passions. The discussion of the passions, which anticipates the treatise on the virtues, follows the initial discussion of happiness and the moral analyses of the will and human acts. This entire section of the *Summa* is permeated with Thomas's claims about the indeterminacy of our orientation to any less-than-ultimate good and about our freedom to pursue apparent goods.

The immediate context of Thomas's statement about cannibalism and bestiality is a discussion of the naturalness or unnaturalness of pleasures, not the morality of human acts or the nature of law. His argument against the claim that all pleasures are natural is an argument that a natural-law theorist would be expected to make, but one that in itself does not entail a theory of natural law. In fact, Thomas concludes the discussion of pleasure by underlining its moral significance with respect to virtue: "Moral goodness or malice depends chiefly on the will . . . and it is chiefly from the end that we discern whether the will is good or evil. Now the end is taken to be that in which the will reposes: and the repose of the will and of every appetite in the good is pleasure. And therefore man is reckoned to be good or bad chiefly according to the pleasure of the human will; *since that man is good and virtuous, who takes pleasure in the works of virtue, and that man evil, who takes pleasure in evil works*" (q. 34, a. 4; emphasis added).

One of the two ways in which something like pleasure can be said to be natural to humans, Thomas observes, is if the thing is somehow related to reason, the distinguishing attribute of human nature. In this respect, "it is natural to man to take pleasure in contemplating the truth and in doing works of virtue" (q. 31, a. 7). In other words, because contemplation and virtuous works are especially rational activities, and because humans have a rational nature, Thomas notes it is quite proper to say that the pleasures of contemplation and virtuous acts are natural. The second way a pleasure can be called natural is if it is related to what is shared by human and animal nature. "And in this sense, that which pertains to the preservation of the body, either as regards the individual, as food, drink, sleep, and the like, or as regards the species, as sexual intercourse, are said to afford man natural pleasure" (ibid.).

The way in which some pleasures are *not* natural, Thomas explains, is when someone takes pleasure in irrational activity or in behavior that causes physical harm without reason: "Something which is not natural to man, either in regard to reason, or in regard to the preservation of the body, becomes connatural to this individual man on account of there being some corruption of nature in him" due to a physical ailment or an evil temperament. So it happens that some individuals find eating earth or coals pleasurable, or they delight in cannibalism or bestiality. Note that Thomas refers the former pleasures to a corruption of the animal nature and the latter pleasures to a defect in reason. That is, Thomas is saying that the pleasures of cannibalism and bestiality are unnatural because they are unreasonable. As we have already seen, the standard of moral reasonableness is virtue.

Thomas's argument here does not attempt to prove the *immorality* of these acts. That is not the immediate issue. Such acts most certainly are immoral, as far as Thomas is concerned, but he is not making that argument here. They are also unnatural, in the sense that they are contrary to reason and virtue, but Thomas's immediate point is that *pleasure* in these acts is unnatural. It is not too farfetched to say that this claim, rather than introducing natural-law reasoning, echoes Thomas's repeated statements that we act for the sake of apparent goods and not necessarily for authentic goods. The claim that Thomas resists, that all pleasures are natural, is parallel to the claim that all apprehended goods are actually good because of the way that the desire for pleasure resembles the tendency to apprehended goods. Thomas himself makes the connection explicit in question 34, concerning the moral evaluation of pleasures, in an argument that not all pleasures are good: "All things seek pleasure in the same way they seek the good: since pleasure is the repose of the appetite in the good. But, just as it happens that not every good which is desired, is of itself and verily good; so not every pleasure is of itself and verily good" (q. 34, a. 2; reply to objection 3).

Thomas's statements about natural pleasures do not support a simple equation of natural and good or unnatural and evil. The relation between the natural and the good is complex in a way that undermines natural law. To say that a pleasure is natural, Thomas has pointed out, is to say it refers either to the animal appetite or to reason. Animal nature can be corrupted by illness, making sweet things, for example, taste bitter. The fact that one finds the taste of sugar bitter, however, is not a matter of choice and thus not morally significant. On the other hand, the sensitive appetite can be corrupted by an evil temperament, making one take pleasure in eating dirt, or the rational part of the soul can be corrupted by a bad custom or habit, making one take pleasure in cannibalism or bestiality (to cite Thomas's examples). These things are subject to choice and therefore not only morally significant but also vicious because they are contrary to reason, which does not in and of itself have any guaranteed apprehension of authentic goodness. Reason has to be made right by virtue.

A virtue or vice, as Thomas is about to point out, is a habitual or customary trait of character. He notes in the next question that whatever is customary "becomes pleasant, in so far as it becomes natural: because custom is like a second nature" (q. 32, a. 2). Because a virtue or vice, a customary trait of behavior, can be considered as a "second" kind of natural attribute, the statement that a morally significant unnatural or natural pleasure is wrong or right can be roughly equivalent to the statement that it is opposed to or accords with virtue. Thomas's observation that some take unnatural delight in cannibalism or bestiality "from custom" and that taking pleasure in virtuous acts is natural (q. 31, a. 7) is significant in this regard. Virtuous acts or pleasures are natural in the sense that they accord with reason, the distinguishing characteristic of the human species, as well as in the sense of being customary. Vicious acts, on the other hand, which are opposed to reason, are natural only in the sense that they are customary to a corrupt nature.

Thomas's use of the adjective "natural" in a moral context, therefore, is not automatically a reference to a determinate set of innate attributes. Thomas's use here of the word "natural" as a reference to generic features is limited to those features that human and animal nature have in common. (This is not to say, however, that those shared features are identical.) In response to the question of whether the passion of anger is more natural than desire, for example, Thomas says that the answer depends on the sense in which natural is used: "If then we consider the generic nature, i.e., the nature of this man considered as an animal; thus desire is more natural than anger; because it is from this very generic nature that man is inclined to desire those things which tend to preserve in him the life both of the species and of the individual" (q. 46, a. 5). This is a restatement of the claim we have seen already—that we share with other living creatures a tendency toward the general conditions of physical existence. We eat, drink, and procreate.

Thomas also uses natural in a wider sense when he refers to the nature of a rational creature, for whom a natural act or pleasure is one that is customary or one that pertains to reason. The pleasure of virtuous activity is natural to an individual through "a man's habitual inclination to do good, by reason of which doing good becomes connatural to him: for which reason the liberal man takes pleasure in giving to others" (q. 32, a. 6). The passion of anger is natural because one has to reason in order to be angry. "Reason itself belongs to the very nature of man: wherefore from the very fact that anger requires an act of reason, it follows that it is, in a manner, natural to man" (q. 46, a. 5). The same could be said of all of the passions Thomas has discussed in the entire treatise.

The fact that some act or pleasure is natural, then, in itself tells us nothing about its goodness or malice. The fact that it is natural to a human to eat as well as to be angry tells us nothing about how to behave. Each action or passion has to be judged according to whether it accords with right reason. The standard for right reason with respect to human behavior is virtue, the subject to which Thomas turns next.

3

THE PRIORITY OF PRUDENCE

*Through prudence we deliberate well about matters pertaining to
the whole of human life and the ultimate end of human life.*
— *Summa Theologica*

I

Thomas's most explicit discussion of the importance of prudence and his
richest description of the relation between prudence and the other moral
virtues occurs in the "Treatise on the Virtues," questions 49–67 of the
Prima Secundae of the *Summa*. This treatise, like the subsequent "Treatise
on Law," should not be read in isolation but rather in the context of the
material leading up to it, which is why I postponed dealing with prudence
directly until I had described the context for prudence. Thomas's teaching about the moral life, his account of our orientation to the good,
his claim about our proper happiness, the description of the role of
circumstances, the analyses of the will and of human acts, and the
portrayal of the passions, have anticipated an ethics of virtue under
the direction of the virtue of prudence. The standard version of an ethics
of natural law does not easily follow from this material, especially considering Thomas's stress on the indeterminacy of our orientation to
particular goods. An ethics of virtue is invited, in contrast, precisely
because our powers of will and intellect are not determined to specific
ends. They need to be ordered and perfected with respect to their proper
good by virtuous habits.

Chapter 2 should have at least raised questions about the grounds for
attributing the standard version of natural law to Thomas, because the
treatises on happiness and the passions do not appear to have provided

any appropriate foundations for such a theory. If one considers Thomas's claims about the role of the virtues and their direction by prudence described in this chapter, the familiar natural-law interpretation is likely to seem especially problematic. If the theory of natural law ordinarily attributed to Thomas has foundations that we have not yet encountered but perhaps shall encounter in the "Treatise on Law," that theory would appear to be at least a puzzling and conflicting addition to the prudential ethics described in the "Treatise on the Virtues" and elsewhere in the *Summa*.

It is not entirely anachronistic when interpreting Thomas's ethics to describe the themes of the virtues and natural law as being in some sort of opposition. After all, Thomas was attempting to integrate an estab- lished natural-law tradition with an Aristotelian tradition of virtue. What is at issue is how to understand Thomas's portrayal of those two traditions. My claim that it is a mistake to attribute an ethics of natural law to Thomas refers to the prevailing version of natural law described earlier in this essay. I am not saying that he was somehow arguing against the very notion of natural law by stressing prudence or that his teaching about natural law has been frequently misrepresented but that prudence and the virtues have priority over natural law in his account of moral under- standing and decision making.

Thomas introduces the discussion of virtue by saying that habits and virtues are the intrinsic principles of human acts while law and grace are their extrinsic principles (1966: *S.T.* I–II, q. 49; subsequent references to the "Treatise on the Virtues" will be to this translation unless otherwise indicated). In order for acts to be our own, and in order for them to have moral significance, they have to originate in us. As we have seen, accord- ing to Thomas, human acts proceed from the various powers of the soul. Habits and virtues, the intrinsic principles of acts, are enabling and perfecting dispositions that prompt those powers to act in a certain way. The "Treatise on the Virtues" is a general discussion of virtuous habits, an overview of their operation and interrelation. (The virtues are considered individually and in detail in the *Secunda Secundae*.)

The "Treatise on the Virtues" is oriented toward the two central virtues of charity and prudence, each of which concerns a level of our proper good as humans. Paul J. Wadell argues convincingly that the virtue of charity, described as friendship with God, is the key to understanding Thomas's treatment of the moral life (Wadell 1985). Wadell's stress on charity is entirely appropriate and does not conflict with my similar claim on behalf of prudence because each virtue has to do with a different aspect of the moral life. Charity, to be sure, is the preeminent and more encompassing virtue because its activity suits us for our final end, ultimate good, and complete happiness. Near the end of the "Treatise on the Virtues" Thomas considers whether the moral virtues can even exist without charity. He says that "insofar as they are productive of good works in relation to a supernatural last end, and thus truly and perfectly attain the nature of virtue, they cannot be acquired by human acts but are infused by God. Moral virtues of this kind cannot exist without charity" (I-II, q. 65, a. 2). Interpreting Thomas's ethics in terms of charity rightly preserves the thoroughly theological cast of Thomas's moral teaching. (See J. M. Gustafson, 1968, 102–9, for a helpful summary of the role of charity in Thomas's thought and of the relation between the theological and moral virtues. For an extensive treatment of the ways in which the cardinal virtues, and especially prudence, are transformed by charity and the theological virtues, see Gerard Gilleman, 1959.)

Thomas is also concerned, however, with what is sometimes called natural virtue, which is not a reference to innate virtue but to the "secondary" or "imperfect" kind of happiness that can be obtained in this life through our own efforts. Happiness of this kind is the fruit of the moral virtues under the direction of prudence. In the same passage in which Thomas affirms the preeminence of charity, he also acknowledges the priority of prudence for attaining the good life within our own reach. Insofar as the moral virtues "are productive of good works ordered to an end which does not surpass the natural capacity of man, [they] can be acquired by human actions" in the absence of charity. These moral virtues, he notes, "cannot exist without prudence nor prudence without the moral virtues inasmuch as the moral virtues make a man well disposed to certain ends, from which the reasoning of prudence proceeds" (I-II, q. 65, a. 2).

A complete interpretation of Thomas's ethics would describe the theological virtues, explain their relation to charity, and discuss the relation between the natural and infused virtues. In particular, a thorough analysis of Thomas's moral teaching would explicate the relation between prudence and charity. From the theological perspective, prudence depends on charity because charity correctly disposes a person to the ultimate end. As Thomas says, "[F]or the right reasoning of prudence it is much more necessary that man be well disposed to the ultimate end, which is the result of charity, than that he be well disposed to the other ends, which is the result of moral virtue." He adds that "infused prudence cannot exist without charity; nor, consequently, the other moral virtues, for they cannot exist without prudence" (I–II, q. 65, a. 2).

This is not the occasion for that kind of all-encompassing completeness. My concern here is a more particular interest in prudence as one of the virtues that Thomas says we can strive to attain on our own and which leads to the kind of natural happiness that is possible in this life. In other words, I am discussing only the kind of virtue, or the level of prudence, that Thomas says can be attained by pagans as well as by Christians. Moreover, I shall not be discussing particular virtues in any detail except to explain their relationship to prudence. My concern is specifically with prudence, and by focusing on prudence I hope to make a two-part claim. In this chapter I shall suggest that Thomas's description of the role of prudence makes the standard version of natural law commonly attributed to him superfluous. A prudential ethics of virtue does not require a supplementary ethics of natural law. I shall go on to argue that Thomas's discussion of natural law can be interpreted in a way that does not involve him in using it as a source of concrete moral information and in a way that does not conflict with the account of prudential ethics described here.

II

In order to understand what prudence is and does, we need to understand more generally what a virtue is and does. One way of attempting to explain virtues would be to enter into a conversation with some contemporary theorists and try to refine the descriptions or definitions that they provide. Gilbert Meilaender's recent book, *The Theory and Practice of Virtue* (1984), begins with an essay called "Thinking about Virtue" that adopts as its starting point a definition provided by Josef Pieper (1965): Virtues are "those excellences which enable a human being 'to attain the furthest potentialities of his nature' " (Meilaender 1984: 6). Meilaender draws on other sources in elaborating that definition, but his main inspiration is Pieper, whom he commends for not engaging in futile methodological disputes and for following his own path of explicating Thomas's teaching about virtue. I propose to recommend rather than rehash Meilaender and Pieper, and to follow Meilaender's suggestion that

Pieper has adopted as good a strategy as any in drawing directly from Thomas. Because an analysis of modern attempts to provide an account of virtue would inevitably lead to an indirect encounter with Thomas, a reasonable way to understand generally what a virtue is and does is to look first at what Thomas says. His description may seem somewhat remote at times, but that is only because what he is describing is somewhat unfamiliar to contemporary culture, not because his powers of description are defective.

He begins his explanation by saying that a virtue is a special kind of habit that, in the Aristotelian scheme of classifying things according to their ultimate genera, is a durable "quality" that disposes a thing for better or worse with respect to itself or something else. Thomas's notion of habit is considerably broader than ours. The first example he gives of a habit is health, which is a good disposition of the body (I-II, q. 49, a. 1). The features of a habit that Thomas stresses are its durability (a habit is a quality that is difficult to change) and its tendency to dispose a thing for good or ill. Just as there are habits of the body, such as health and sickness, there are also habits of the soul, which will turn out to be virtues and vices.

The kinds of habits with which Thomas is especially concerned in order to explain the virtues are those that dispose us in a good or poor way with respect to the passions (ibid., a. 2). These habits are located in the powers of the soul and "order" us toward acts, Thomas says. He grants that the primary feature of a habit is its disposition of a thing in a way "appropriate or inappropriate" to its nature, which may not involve any action on the part of the agent at all. But because Thomas is concerned with moral habits, he singles out for attention the habits that perfect the powers of the soul for action. A thing acts through its powers, he notes, and the habits located in those powers are oriented toward action: "If, then, the nature of the thing in which habit is, consists in this ordering toward act, it follows that habit principally implies an ordering toward act. Now it is clear that it is of the nature and notion of a power that it be the principle of an act. Hence every habit which is in a power as in a subject principally implies an ordering toward an act" (ibid., a. 3).

Habits are necessary for rational creatures because we are not determined in any one way and because our powers can be used for good or for evil. Habits are enabling dispositions. If we could act in only one way through our intellectual and appetitive powers, and if we inevitably employed our powers appropriately, we would act automatically and effortlessly and habits would be superfluous. Habits are *not* necessary, Thomas says, when "a thing is disposed to something in such a way that it is in potency only to that" because "such a subject of its very nature has a disposition sufficient for such an act." The human soul, however, has a "form" which "is such that it can act in diverse ways" and thus "must be disposed for its its activities by certain habits." In order to be perfected, in order to act in an appropriate way, the soul requires good habits, the virtues (ibid., a. 4). Habits are necessary because their subject, the soul, "is in potentiality to many things" (I-II, q. 50, a. 1) and needs to be ordered or determined by way of an acquired "second nature" in a direction toward which it is not naturally determined.

When Thomas says that the habits ordered to operation *perfect* the powers of the soul (I-II, q. 54, a. 4), he does not only mean that they make possible the attainment of some difficult ideal. The virtues do indeed dispose a person toward the attainment of the ideal good, and in that sense they do aim toward one notion of perfection. More basically, however, when something is perfected it is completed. Something that is perfected is not beyond the norm of its operation but rather is enabled to operate normally. To say that a power is completed or perfected is to say that it has been made to operate at its full capacity, to function as it ought to function. Habits, then, are not only necessary to give the powers of the soul direction, but also to permit them to work well. Without habits, according to Thomas, we cannot even act in a truly human fashion.

The standard natural-law interpretation tends to present a watered-down theory of the virtues in which they function merely to motivate agents toward naturally known ends. According to Thomas's account, although virtuous habits certainly have an important motivating role, their importance is much more central. The nature of a power, according to Thomas, is to be "in potency" to act. Without habits, our powers, lacking natural determination to concrete ends, are merely potentials without specific direction. When the form of something "is such that it can act in diverse ways, as is the case with the soul, it must be disposed for its activities by certain habits" (I-II, q. 49, a. 4). The powers of the soul, lacking direction of their own, are "related to good and evil. Hence habits are necessary to determine the powers to good activity" (ibid.).

Thomas locates the habits of temperance and fortitude in the sensitive powers of the soul, insofar as they can be commanded by reason and thus are not determined, and locates the habits of wisdom, science, and understanding in the intellect (I-II, q. 50, aa. 3-4). The rational will in particular is the subject of the habit of justice because the will is especially undetermined and in need of ordering to a determinate good. Thomas says the will is "diversely ordered as far as its act is concerned" precisely because it is a *rational* appetitive power (I-II, q. 50, a. 5). The nature of the will is to incline to the good, but it inclines to the apparent good presented to it by reason. The will is not ordered to act in a single way, but it needs to be directed in order for us to act and live well. Because "it is necessary in relation to what human life is ordered to, that the appetitive power be inclined to something determinate, to which it is not inclined by its nature—being related to many and diverse things," the will and other powers of appetite need to be ordered and perfected by a habit that inclines "to a good determined by reason" (ibid.). Reason, as we shall see, does not operate autonomously in determining the good, but is perfected for that task by the virtue of prudence, which directs the activity of various virtues.

Habits (and by extension, virtues and vices) are caused by action (I-II, q. 51, a. 2). We have forgotten or abandoned much of Thomas's positive conception of habits, but this is the same claim we regularly make about bad habits. An action repeated often enough becomes habitual, and by becoming habitual it becomes easy—in the case of bad habits, all too easy. Good habits are like skills, which take the practice of repeated acts to develop. Thomas explains that the development of a habitual quality in the passive will depends on the gradual and cumulative effect of the active principle of reason. The will does not move on its own, but only as reason judges. It takes more than one act for reason, which "judges in a single act that this should be willed for these reasons and in these circumstances," to dominate the indeterminately ordered will and cause the habit (I-II, q. 51, a. 3). Similarly, virtues are lost by acting contrary to the habit, not just on one occasion, but repeatedly, or by not acting at all (I-II, q. 53, aa. 2-3).

Thomas also says that there is a way in which habits are caused by nature, and the example he gives is the habit of understanding first principles (I-II, q. 51, a. 1). Obviously, this proposition is directly relevant to the question of the relative importance of prudence and natural law. Before examining what Thomas might mean by the claim that we have natural knowledge of first principles, I would like to look more specifically at what he says about prudence and the cardinal virtues.

III

In order to appreciate the importance of prudence, we need to understand something about the importance and role of the other virtues because Thomas portrays prudence as both ordering and dependent on the other cardinal virtues of temperance, justice, and fortitude. We have seen that Thomas describes virtues as durable habits directed toward action, which are caused or diminished by acting or not acting, and which are located in and perfective of the rational and appetitive powers of the soul. His basic definition of a virtue, elaborated and restated in various ways, is that it is "a good quality [or habit] of the mind, by which we live rightly, of which no one can make bad use" (I-II, q. 55, a. 4). He also says that a virtue is "the good use of free choice" (I-II, q. 55, a. 1) and "an ordering of love" (ibid.). A virtue is "that which makes a thing's work be done well" (I-II, q. 55, a. 2), "an ordered disposition of the soul" (ibid.), and "operation in conformity with right reason" (I-II, q. 56, a. 2). It is useful to think of virtues as skills for living well, but what distinguishes a virtue from a skill is that a virtue is responsible for the goodness of an action as well as the goodness of the agent: A virtue is "that which makes the one who has it good and the work which he does good" (I-II, q. 55, a. 3).

Virtues vary according to the powers that they perfect and with which they are associated, Thomas says. There is a class of intellectual virtues that governs our rational powers (I-II, q. 56, a. 3), which can be ordered to either speculative or practical activity. The speculative activity of the intellect depends on the virtues of wisdom, science, and understanding (I-II, q. 57, a. 2), while the intellect's practical activity, its reasoning about things to be made or done, depends on the virtues of art and prudence. The intellectual virtues (with the notable exception of prudence) are not virtues "simply" but only in a restricted way, or only insofar as they are subject to a virtuous will, because they confer an ability or aptitude to act well without guaranteeing the inclination to do so. There also is a class of moral virtues that governs the appetitive powers insofar as they are subject to reason (I-II, q. 56, a. 4). Thomas says that these moral virtues associated with the will are virtues in the most basic sense because they not only make an activity good but also make the person who is acting good:

> But the subject of a habit which is called [a] virtue simply can only be the will, or some power as moved by the will. This is

because the will moves to their acts all other powers that are in some way rational, as we have said. Hence if a man actually acts well, this is a result of his having a good will. Therefore, the virtue which makes a man actually act well, not merely have the ability to act well, must be in the will or in some power as it is moved by the will. (I-II, q. 56, a. 3)

The most important virtues of the sort that rectify the will are the cardinal virtues of temperance, fortitude, justice, and prudence (which is a moral and intellectual virtue). Although the subject of the intellectual virtues (the intellect) ranks higher according to Thomas than the subject of the moral virtues (the will), the moral virtues rank higher as virtues because they most directly concern the appetite's orientation to the good (I-II, q. 61, a. 1). Temperance, which governs the concupiscible appetite, restrains the passions when they tend to something opposed to reason, while fortitude, which governs the irascible appetite, strengthens the passions when they shrink from the danger or difficulty of doing something that reason commands (I-II, q. 61, a. 2). Justice, which governs the will, orders the will with respect to its operations concerning others, "for example, in buying and selling, and other actions of the kind which involve a consideration of what is owed or not owed to another (I-II, q. 60, a. 2). All the moral virtues seek what Thomas says is a good of reason or a good determined by reason. The cardinal virtue that seeks a good "as realized in the very act of reasoning" is prudence, which perfects the practical activity of reason and directs the other virtues (I-II, q. 61, a. 2).

These four virtues are cardinal or principal, according to Thomas, because they contain all the other virtues or because all the other virtues share in them. He says this is why any restraint of the passions is called temperance, any strengthening of the soul is called fortitude, any achievement of what is due to another is called justice, and any perfection of rational deliberation is called prudence (I-II, q. 61, a. 3). Thomas also claims these four are the principal virtues because considered as specific virtues their actual concerns are primary compared to the concerns of other virtues: Temperance governs the pleasures of touch, fortitude governs the fear of death, justice has to do with relations between equals, and prudence commands action. Although each of the four cardinal virtues is "principal in its own genus," he adds, prudence is "more principal" than the others (I-II, q. 61, a. 3).

The distinction Thomas makes between prudence and art, the other virtue perfecting the practical intellect, helps to illustrate how far the modern conception of prudence has departed from the classical notion. According to a common modern view, prudence has to do with the self-interested calculation of costs and benefits. We tend to think of prudence as a kind of calculating carefulness, an ability to anticipate consequences. We might even presume a prudent person to be clever in considering possibly illicit means to ends that are not necessarily good. We see it as a trait that can be as characteristic of a master criminal as a law-abiding citizen. In fact, we often view prudence negatively and associate it with people who know what is right but refrain from doing it because of their concern for the expected costs. The modern estimation of prudence has come to mistake for genuine prudence what Thomas calls the "vices opposed to prudence by way of resemblance": prudence of the flesh (which views carnal goods as the ultimate end of life), craftiness (which employs illicit means), guile (which executes illicit means through deceptive words), fraud (which executes illicit means through deceptive deeds), oversolicitousness for temporal matters, and oversolicitousness for the future (1947: *S.T.* II-II, q. 55, aa. 1-7; all subsequent references to II-II are to this edition).

For Thomas, the ability to reason about action in the absence of an appetite for the good is more like an art, while prudence produces not only the ability to act well but also presumes the desire. Thomas says that the "reason for this difference is that art is *right reasoning about what is to be made* whereas prudence is *right reasoning about what is to be done*" (I-II, q. 57, a. 4; emphasis in original). Art and prudence, which concern contingent things, are different from intellectual virtues of wisdom, knowledge, and understanding, which concern necessary things. They are distinct from each other, however, in that art has to do "with things produced in external matter" while prudence is "concerned with things done, that is, with things that have their being in the doer himself" (II-II, q. 47, a. 5). Making is an exterior affair, but *doing* is something that produces not only an action but also "is an activity remaining within the agent" (I-II, q. 57, a. 4). The reason *doing* is distinguished from *making* in being so intimately associated with the agent is not only that we develop habits through doing, but also that any morally significant deed proceeds from the will's orientation to the good. In practical reasoning, Thomas says, the ends we perceive as good are equivalent to principles in speculative reasoning. Instead of proceeding straightforwardly from principles, right reasoning about doing requires that a person "be well disposed in regard to ends, and this depends on right appetite. Hence, for prudence, one must have moral virtue, which rectifies the appetite" (ibid.).

Obviously, making something can be a morally significant deed. Thomas's point in distinguishing prudence from art, however, is that the virtue of art only perfects the artisan's ability to make something well. Art does not perfect the artisan as a moral agent. This is why, he notes, intentional mistakes on the part of an artisan are sometimes praiseworthy and not contrary to art while willful error is entirely opposed to prudence. Authentic prudence presupposes a good will. One can talk about prudent soldiers and prudent sea captains and even prudent criminals, but to do so is to use the term loosely. The prudence of robbers is false prudence because it seeks efficient means to evil ends. The prudence of soldiers, sailors, or businessmen is a kind of prudence, but it is imperfect or incomplete. It seeks the best means to an end, but the end is particular and limited to the goods peculiar to a certain vocation rather than the "common end" of human "life as a whole" (II–II, q. 47, a. 13). To say that someone is prudent in an unqualified way is to say that he or she is prudent about life in general. "Through prudence we deliberate well about matters pertaining to the whole of human life and the ultimate end of human life," Thomas claims, and "[o]nly those who deliberate well about matters concerning the whole of human life are called prudent without qualification" (ibid.).

Prudence is obtained and perfected through practice in deliberation and action, just as the virtue of temperance, for example, is cultivated through acting temperately. Although Thomas acknowledges a divinely infused prudence, the cardinal virtue of acquired prudence is dependent on one's experience in moral deliberation over a lifetime, which is why it is seldom found in the young (II–II, q. 47, a. 14). "Prudence is rather in the old," Thomas says, "not only because their natural disposition calms the movement of the sensitive passions" that hinder reasoning about action, "but also because of their long experience" (II–II, q. 47, a. 15). In fact, Thomas is entirely willing to follow Aristotle in saying we ought to attend to even the *undemonstrated* claims and opinions of those who are older, and thus presumably more experienced and prudent than we are, because their long life has given them an understanding of moral principles (II–II, q. 49, a. 2).

Although there are practical principles and rules of thumb reflecting the accumulated moral wisdom of a community or culture to which one can look for guidance in moral decision-making, one does not become prudent by memorizing a set of principles. One could study the just-war tradition, for example, and become familiar with the criteria that war be waged for a just cause, with just authority, with just intentions, by just means, that it be a last resort, that there be reasonable hope of success, and that there be a proper proportionality of good to evil effects, yet still be unable to make a prudent assessment of whether a particular war is just or not. This is precisely the point expressed by Jeffrey Stout in an unpublished essay that draws on Thomas's account of prudential moral reasoning for an analysis of the ethics of war:

> If moral understanding is an ability, it must be an acquired ability, the kind of skill young children evidently lack but most of us, with any luck, achieve at least in some degree. It is a skilled habit directed toward the good—in short, a virtue to be nurtured. The Wittgensteinian thought that understanding is an acquired skill brings us back to the traditional virtue of prudence and to the cardinal importance of education and community.
>
> But acquiring the virtue of prudence, of genuine moral understanding and sensitivity, involves more than learning how to apply principles to cases, if by application we mean a process that always leaves the principles themselves unchanged. It also involves, in no small measure, acquiring the ability to reinterpret and revise principles when circumstances dictate: the virtue of knowing how and when to change one's mind about relatively abstract and general moral propositions in the light of lived moral experience. To be sure, it involves much else besides, much of which has little or nothing to do with principles. (Stout 1985)

Prudence enables our rational activities of deliberation and choosing to be done well. Thomas describes it as an application of "right reason to action" (II–II, q. 47, a. 4) and as "wisdom about human affairs" (II–II, q. 47, a. 1). Its concerns are essentially practical. Although one can speak about a prudent natural or social scientist (insofar as the scientist is a prudent individual) prudence is concerned with contingent rather than necessary truths. In the realm of action, the means to ends are not pre-determined by the natures of things. Although prudence appropriately directs the application of speculative knowledge or art, prudence is not

properly a speculative virtue. Thomas observes that because "the speculative reason makes things such as syllogisms, propositions and the like,
wherein the process follows certain and fixed rules, consequently in
respect of such things it is possible to have the essentials of art, but not
of prudence; and so we find such a thing as a speculative art, but not a
speculative prudence" (II–II, q. 47, a. 2).

Prudence is a necessary virtue for practical reasoning because it
enables one to do good deeds, the activity in which a good life consists,
and to become a good and happy person. For a deed to be truly good,
Thomas explains, it has to be done in the right way and for the right
reasons. Harming a man out of anger, for example, would be opposed
to justice as well as to prudence, while harming a man to prevent him
from maliciously injuring an innocent victim could well be a prudential
act of virtue. Prudence enables us to act in the right way, for the right
reasons, and at the right time. It seeks to discern what is to be done now
or in the future on the basis of knowledge of the present situation and
past experience. Prudence gives one a sense of moral perspective. A
prudent individual "considers things afar off, in so far as they tend to be
a help or hindrance to that which has to be done at the present time"
(II–II, q. 47, a. 1).

The activity of prudence depends on a variety of subsidiary skills or
habits as well as on some auxiliary virtues. Thomas says the chief acts of
prudence are "rightly to counsel, judge, and command concerning the
means of obtaining a due end" (II–II, q. 47, a. 10). In other words, prudence
is a perfected habit of inquiring about an action through good counsel
or deliberation, of making a judgment about the results of the inquiry,
and especially of commanding appropriate action on the basis of one's
counsel and judgment (II–II, q. 47, a. 8). We choose what to do, Thomas
says, on the basis of what has been counseled, and a prudent person is
one who is good at taking counsel or deliberating (II–II, q. 47, a. 1).

Although there is a divine gift of counsel corresponding to prudence
(II–II, q. 52, a. 2), Thomas is concerned here with an acquired virtue of
counsel or deliberation, distinct from prudence although directed towards
it, which has the Greek name *eubulia* (II–II, q. 51, a. 2; I–II, q. 57, a. 6).
Thomas presents the related capacity of good judgment as being perfected
by the two distinct virtues of *synesis* and *gnome*. *Synesis* is a cognitive
faculty of good judgment or "sagacity" with reference to commonly
accepted norms of behavior (I–II, q. 57, a. 6). It perfects our capacity for
"apprehending a thing just as it is in reality" (II–II, q. 51, a. 3). In other

words, prudential judgment depends on an ability to size up a situation and see it as it actually is, an ability to discern that some concrete course of action counts as a case of ordinarily forbidden, commanded, or permitted behavior. *Gnome* also perfects our judgment about action, but it refers to the ability to judge what is right in terms of equity when the ordinary rules and guidelines do not apply or appear to be in conflict (II-II, q. 51, a. 4; I-II, q. 57, a. 6).

Prudence also includes as "integral parts" the habits of "[m]emory, intelligence, and foresight, as well as caution, docility, and the like" (I-II, q. 57, a. 6). A person's judgment about human actions cannot be guided "by those things that are simply and necessarily true," according to Thomas's account, but rather by knowledge of what is right and true most of the time. Good judgment in contingent affairs, the concern of prudence, is a matter of experience developed over time, requiring a good memory from which experience can draw (II-II, q. 49, a. 1). In addition to the ability to understand and apply general principles of action, prudence also depends on a good understanding and estimate of the concrete and particular features of individual situations, the "primary singular and contingent practical matter" that makes a specific act what it is (ibid., a. 2). Because the features of actions and their attendant circumstances are so variable, however, even the good judgment of a richly experienced individual is often inadequate to give them due consideration within a reasonable amount of time. Prudence indeed requires a certain shrewdness, which is the ability to estimate correctly about the features of actions on one's own (ibid., a. 4), but a person also "stands in very great need of being taught by others," which requires docility (ibid., a. 3).

Shrewdness combined with alertness "to do whatever has to be done" is a part of prudence that Thomas calls solicitude, which enables a person to deliberate as long as necessary to reach a correct judgment but then to act decisively when action is called for (ibid., a. 9). The development of prudence also depends on the ability to reason well (ibid., a. 5), to anticipate the future variables of action through the capacity of foresight or providence (ibid., a. 6), and to consider the suitability of means to ends in light of the actual circumstances of a situation, which requires circumspection (ibid., a. 7). Caution, although far from being equivalent to prudence, is a necessary adjunct in order to guard against those things that one anticipates will impede virtue or to prepare as well as possible for dealing with unanticipated accidents (ibid., a. 8).

In addition to individual or what Thomas calls "monastic" prudence, there are also different kinds of prudence that perfect reasoning about action in contexts other than the pursuit of the good for an individual's life. Thomas is not entirely consistent in his enumeration of the various species of prudence, and as we have seen, he sometimes talks as if only the kind of prudence that refers to the conduct of a person's life as a whole is authentic prudence. Yet he states straightforwardly that there is also a true form of prudence that is oriented to public rather than private life. "[S]ince it belongs to prudence rightly to counsel, judge, and command concerning the means of obtaining a due end," he points out, "it is evident that prudence regards not only the private good of the individual, but also the common good of the multitude" (II-II, q. 47, a. 10). He calls this political or "regnative" prudence, which is associated with the governance of a kingdom for the common good (ibid., a. 11; II-II, q. 50, a. 1). Prudence's perfection of deliberation, judgment, and command with respect to the common good is a feature that all the various kinds of prudence share. Some forms consider the common good explicitly, while others, including individual prudence, consider particular goods in light of the general good of the community. A special form of political pru-dence concerns a subject's obedience to a superior "in relation to the common good (II-II, q. 50, a. 2). The military arts, to the extent that they pertain to the preservation and defense of the common good, are also governed by prudence (ibid., a. 4). Intermediate between the public and private forms of prudence is domestic prudence, which directs the affairs of a household for the common good of a family (ibid., a. 3; II-II, q. 57, a. 11).

Virtues are characteristically opposed by corresponding vices, and prudence is no exception. By noting what Thomas says prudence is not, it is possible to see clearly what ought to characterize practical deliberation. Prudence is opposed by the especially imprudent sins of precipitation, thoughtlessness, inconstancy, and negligence (II-II, q. 53, aa. 3–5; q. 54). A prudent person deliberates in a measured and careful way, judges circumstances accurately by attending to all their relevant features, consistently resists the undue influence of the passions in the pursuit of the good, and completes deliberation and judgment by commanding the performance of an appropriate action.

For prudence to be perfected, however, it is not enough for its various component and auxiliary abilities to be in place and polished by long experience. Because prudence is a virtue and not reducible to a skill or an art, according to Thomas, it depends on some sustaining vision of what constitutes a complete, successful, perfected, and good life. Essentially it is an intellectual virtue, because it perfects a rational power and has the practical activity of the intellect as its subject. But Thomas also considers it to be a moral virtue "as regards its matter"—the will's orientation toward things to be done—which it shares with the other moral virtues (I-II, q. 58, a. 3).

The activities of prudence, which perfects the practical intellect, and of the moral virtues, which perfect the will, can be distinguished for purposes of analysis but cannot be separated in practice. The two things that Thomas says are necessary for our choice of deeds to be correct are a good end, to which we are disposed through the moral virtues, and "something suitably ordered to that end," to which we are disposed by prudence (I-II, q. 57, a. 5). A good action does not proceed only from temperance or only from prudence, for example, but depends on both. Thomas says that "in order that a man's actions be good, not only must his reason be well disposed by a habit of intellectual virtue, but also his appetitive power by a habit of moral virtue" (I-II, q. 58, a. 2). In other words, the activities of prudence and the other cardinal virtues are interdependent. The moral virtues depend on prudence, which makes for good choices, and prudence depends on the moral virtues, which direct it toward the good. One of the objections Thomas considers to his claim that prudence is principally a cognitive and not an appetitive virtue quotes Augustine's statement that "[p]rudence is love choosing wisely between things that help and those that hinder." Thomas replies that our loves, or our appetites, and prudence are intertwined. Love has a rational aspect because it prompts reasoning and deliberation, while prudence has an appetitive aspect because it is moved to act by love (II-II, q. 47, a. 1).

Through the moral virtues we intend good ends, and through prudent deliberation, judgment, and command of action we are able to attain them. As we have already seen, the distinction between ends and means is far from absolute. Because Thomas believes there is one ultimate end to which every other good end is ordered, every end but the final end can also be viewed as a means to a further end. Prudence, strictly speaking, is concerned with the means toward ends to which we are oriented by the moral virtues. The moral virtues, however, depend for their direction on the ordering and control of prudence. Through prudence we deliberate about means toward ends, but our orientation to ends themselves also is subject to the prudent direction of reason. Thomas says that "the whole matter of moral virtue falls under the direction of prudence" (I-II, q. 65, a. 1). The moral virtues do not order us to the good apart from the activity of prudential reason, and prudence does not perfect rational deliberation in the absence of an orientation to particular goods. Prudence depends on the moral virtues for its principles, and "the moral virtues . . . depend on prudence inasmuch as the appetite in a way moves reason, and reason appetite" (I-II, q. 65, a. 2).

One of the ways in which Thomas expresses this thorough interdependence of the moral virtues and prudence is through his observation that the goodness of moral virtue consists in its conformity to the rule of reason or to a mean. Virtue perfects the appetite with respect to the good, Thomas says, but "the measure" or "rule" of the appetite is reason. In other words, the appetite's tendency to a particular end is good if it conforms to reason, and its tendency is evil if it exceeds or falls short of the measure established by reason. The conformity to reason that makes the appetite good is "the mean between excess and a defect" (I-II, q. 64, a. 1). Determining the mean of the governance of the passions by virtue requires the judgment of prudence because "[t]he mean and extremes in actions and passions depend on the differing circumstances" (ibid.). That is, prudential reason has to take account of *where* an action is right, "*when* it is right, and *why* it is right" (ibid.; emphasis in original).

The moral virtues direct us to good ends, and prudence depends on their ordering of our appetite for the substance of its deliberations, but the virtues depend on prudence for their reasonableness. The virtue of fortitude, for example, is not disregard for danger under just any circumstances, but it allows one to fear only those dangers that ought to be feared and only to the degree that they should be feared. Fortitude is a mean, established by prudence, between timidity and fearlessness. There is no true courage, nor any other authentically moral virtue, without prudence. According to Thomas, "[p]rudence directs the moral virtues not only in choosing the means to an end, but also in prescribing the end. Now the end of any moral virtue is to attain the mean in the proper manner, which mean prudence determines by right reasoning" (I-II, q. 66, a. 3).

No other intellectual virtue besides prudence presupposes or requires moral virtue, because the intellectual habits of science, understanding, wisdom, and art can operate perfectly well in the absence of a will directed toward the good. Prudence, however, is precisely concerned with the attainment of the good. (I-II, q. 58, aa. 4-5). One of Thomas's most explicit statements about the reciprocal relationship between prudence and the moral virtues occurs near the end of the "Treatise on Happiness" where he argues that all the moral virtues are connected through prudence:

[T]here can be no moral virtue without prudence since it belongs to moral virtue, as an elective habit, to make a right choice. Now right choice requires not only an inclination to an appropriate end, which arises directly from the habit of moral virtue, but also the correct choice of means to the end, which is made by prudence, which deliberates, judges, and commands in regard to the means. Likewise, one cannot have prudence without having the moral virtues since prudence is right reasoning about things to be done, whose starting point is the end of action, to which we are rightly disposed by the moral virtues. Hence, just as we cannot have a speculative science without understanding its principles so we cannot have prudence unless we have the moral virtues. (I-II, q. 65, a. 1)

IV

We have seen that for Thomas the measure or rule of the virtues is reason and that practical reason is perfected by the intellectual and moral virtue of prudence, which Thomas describes as right reason about human action. We have also seen that prudence does not operate autonomously or apart from some apprehension of the good but depends on the way in which the virtues order our will to good ends. Furthermore, the distinction between ends, the concern of the moral virtues, and means, the domain of prudence, is not nearly as sharp as some versions of Thomas's ethics suggest. Every end is also a means to a further end, and the moral virtues themselves are dependent on prudence in their very activity of directing us toward the good. The virtues perfect our will, and our desire for goods is a result of the combined activity of our rational and appetitive powers perfected by intellectual and moral virtues.

At this point, one might well ask what Thomas proposes as the "measure" or "truth" of practical reason. The picture sketched above seems to suggest that just as reason is the measure of the virtues, the virtues are the measure of practical reason. In other words, an action is right if it conforms to a virtuous habit, a habit is truly virtuous if it conforms to reason, and the prudential judgments of practical reason are right or true if they are in accord with virtue. The same description could be given of the rightness or goodness of the will as for the rightness of an action: The will is good if it conforms to virtue, the measure of virtue is reason, and reason is right if it is virtuous. Although this circle has to do with virtue, it is a circle nonetheless. Does Thomas step out of the circle and identify some independent measure of the truth or goodness of practical reason?

At one level, the answer is obviously yes because Thomas believes at least part of God's eternal moral law to have been revealed in scripture, and in that sense the judgments of practical reason are true if they conform to that expression of God's will. We can bracket that answer, however, and ask whether Thomas suggests that unaided reason is able to lift itself out of the circle of the reciprocal relationship between moral virtue and prudence and provide its own independent standard of judgment. According to the standard natural-law interpretation of Thomas's ethics, the answer is yes again because reason has the natural capacity to apprehend the first principles of the moral law through the activity of synderesis. According to the reading of Thomas that I have been presenting, however, the answer is no because of what Thomas says about the indeterminacy of our natural inclination to the good.

My task now is to explain that negative answer in more detail, especially in light of his explicit statements that we have a natural knowledge of the first principles of practical reason. I do not believe Thomas is guilty of radical inconsistency or that he has failed to integrate the natural-law tradition as he received it with an Aristotelian ethics of virtue. So far, I have argued that the conventional natural-law interpretation is an inadequate account of Thomas's ethics. That is not to say that Thomas never talks in natural-law terms. The contrast I draw is between an ethics of virtue centered on prudence and an ethics of natural law that deduces moral imperatives from an array of naturally known first principles. Thomas does have a theory of natural law, as I have acknowledged, but his understanding and use of natural law differs considerably from what is ordinarily attributed to him. If one approaches the "Treatise on Law" and certain passages in the treatises on happiness and the virtues without attending to Thomas's larger portrayal of the moral life, the standard natural-law reading appears entirely plausible. But if we now approach that same material after having been acquainted with the context for prudence and with Thomas's claims on behalf of prudence and the virtues, an alternative reading appears more likely. The textual evidence suggests that Thomas only steps outside of the circle circumscribing prudence and virtues to locate the starting point of practical reasoning and perhaps to explain moral agreement, certainly a more striking feature of moral experience in his day than in ours. But natural law does not provide moral guidance. For that, an ethics of virtue is sufficient, at least as far has the happiness of this life is concerned.

Thomas introduces the notion of natural knowledge of first principles of practical reasoning in the "Treatise on the Virtues" when he responds to the question of whether or not we possess any habits by nature. "Included among the various habits is the understanding of principles," he replies, "and this habit is from nature; and this is the reason that first principles are said to be naturally known" (I-II, q. 51, a. 1).

Before stating exactly what he means by this statement he provides some explanatory information. He says that there are two ways in which something can be said to be natural to humans. A thing can be natural to the *species*, for instance the ability to laugh, and something can also be in keeping with a particular *individual's* nature, such as physical health or sickliness. In addition, that something is natural to an individual can mean either that it is wholly or partly from nature. Thomas's example of something wholly natural to an individual is the recovery of health without help, and his example of something partly natural is the recovery of health with the help of the "exterior principle" of medicine. A habit can be natural to the form or nature of a human subject in all of these ways, he points out. Every member of the human species shares a certain disposition that is "proper" and "natural with respect to the nature of the species." He then immediately adds that there is a great deal of variety and "gradation" in that disposition from individual to individual and that the disposition can be either wholly or partly from nature (I-II, q. 51, a. 1). Remember that Thomas's notion of a habit is much broader than ours. A habit is any settled disposition of a subject. What he is saying here is merely that humans are members of a recognizable species with dispositions distinct from members of other species. To that extent, some habits are natural. Granted that there are some general dispositions that all humans share, there is considerable diversity in individual ways of being human.

Thomas next talks specifically about the habit disposing us for operation, or action, which he says is natural to the species, insofar as its subject is a power of the soul, as well as to individuals, insofar as our capacity for operation can vary according to our bodily dispositions (I-II, q. 51, a. 1). In other words, humans share an ability to act (in the moral sense of act that Thomas has already specified) that is influenced for better or worse by our individual makeup. For example, we might observe that some people naturally find it easier to be temperate in the use of alcohol, food, or tobacco than others, or that some people have more intellectual endowments than others and are thus better equipped to reason about actions. But neither with respect to the species nor to the individual, Thomas says, is it the case that operative habits are entirely natural. They are partly from nature and partly due to some other principle (ibid.).

Thomas points out that there is a difference between partly natural habits of the knowing powers and partly natural habits of the appetitive powers. As far as the knowing powers are concerned, some habits common to the species as well as habits peculiar to individuals have a natural *beginning*:

> In regard to the nature of the species, this takes place on the part of the soul; as the understanding of principles, for instance, is said to be a natural habit. For it is owing to the very nature of the intellectual soul that man, as soon as he grasps what a whole is and what a part is, at once knows that every [quantitative] whole is greater than its part, and so with other instances. But what a whole is and what a part is he cannot know except by means of the intelligible species taken from phantasms; and because of this the Philosopher shows that knowledge of principles comes to us via the senses [*Posterior Analytics* II, 19]. In regard to the individual nature, a habit of knowing is natural by way of a beginning insofar as one man, by organic disposition, is more apt than another to understand well, inasmuch as we need sense powers for the operation of our intellect. (I–II, q. 51, a. 1)

There are several important things to note about this statement, which at first glance might seem to provide a foundation for the standard version of natural law associated with Thomas. First of all, Thomas is not speaking specifically about practical knowledge, but about the knowing powers in general. His example of the natural habit of understanding principles, common to the human species, refers to one of the first principles of speculative knowledge, that every whole is greater than its parts. This habit, moreover, is not wholly natural in origin. Thomas cites it as an illustration of a habit that owes its existence "partly to nature and partly to an extrinsic principle" (ibid.). Principles of this sort are not known

automatically. We are not born knowing that a whole is greater than
a part. We might say that such knowledge depends on the acquisition
of a language and on the learned ability to employ the terms "whole"
and "part." Thomas says that the knowledge that a whole is greater than
a part depends on experience. One must have experienced via the sense
powers what a whole is and what a part is before one can have the
corresponding concepts, and only then does one know a whole to be
greater than a part. In short, the claim is merely that humans share the
"natural" capacity to form certain very general concepts of understanding
the world they inhabit and perceive through their senses. Having perceived parts and wholes, for example, we know the quantitative relationship between them. Thomas then goes on to say that this kind of
ability varies from individual to individual. Some of us "naturally" form
concepts more easily than others. The important point to note is that
naturally known principles do not exist in reason apart from experience.
They have more to do with a natural human ability than to formulated
knowledge.

Next, Thomas further qualifies the sense in which appetitive habits can
be said to be natural, but in doing so he makes an easily misunderstood
statement about the principles of common law having something to do
with the origin of the virtues:

> In appetitive powers, however, no habit is natural as to its begin-
> ning on the part of the soul itself, as far as the substance of
> habit is concerned, but only as far as certain of its principles
> are concerned; as the principles of common law, for instance,
> are said to be "seeds of virtues." And this is because the inclina-
> tion to proper objects, which seems to be the beginning of habit,
> does not belong to the habit but rather to the very nature of
> the powers. But on the part of the body, as regards the individual
> nature, there are some appetitive habits by way of natural be-
> ginnings. For some persons are disposed by their bodily tempera-
> ment to chastity or to gentleness, or something of this kind. (I-II,
> q. 51, a. 1)

The meaning of part of this statement is clearly that as far as the
human species is concerned there are not any substantive appetitive
habits "by nature," although some individuals are temperamentally inclined
to have a comparatively easier time than others in forming particular

habits. But what does Thomas mean by saying that "principles" of some habits, as opposed to their substance, are natural to the species, at least as far as their beginnings? The Latin text reads:

In appetitivis autem potentiis non est aliquis habitus naturalis secundum inchoationem, ex parte ipsius animae, quantum ad ipsam substantiam habitus: sed solum quantum ad principia quaedam ipsius, sicut principia juris communis dicuntur esse seminalia virtutum. Et hoc ideo, quia inclinatio ad objecta propria, quae videtur esse inchoatio habitus non pertinet ad habitum, sed magis pertinet ad ipsam rationem potentiarum. (I-II, q. 51, a. 1)

The new Blackfriars edition of the *Summa* offers this alternative translation and an interpretation that is somewhat misleading:

In the appetitive faculties on the other hand there are no dispositions belonging to the soul which are essentially present even in a rudimentary state, but only some preparatory elements, like the principles of natural right which people call "the seeds of virtue" [editor's note: In 1a2ae. 63, 1, St. Thomas says that the seeds of the intellectual and moral virtues are the naturally known principles of knowledge and action. But these principles reside in the intellect, not the will; so here he must mean something similar to what he says in 1a2ae. 27, 3, viz. that all men have the seeds of virtue in the sense that though not virtuous in themselves they admire virtue in others.] This is because the tendency of faculties to their proper objects, which seems like a rudimentary disposition, is not really a disposition at all but something which follows from the very notion of the faculties in question. (Ibid.)

I do not think we need to suppose, as the editor suggests, that Thomas has suddenly shifted in mid-sentence from a discussion of appetitive to intellectual habits. Even if he had, however, his claim would only be that the soul is prepared to develop virtues in accord with the most general principles of natural law. If this were Thomas's meaning, the content of those principles would still remain an open question. There is a much simpler interpretation: Perhaps Thomas is not saying that the "principles" or "preparatory elements" of virtue naturally present in the *appetitive* powers *are* the first principles of common law (here the Blackfriars translation of *juris communis* as "natural right" is misleading) but only that they *resemble* those principles.

The resemblance is instructive. The thrust of the argument concerns the relative insignificance of the natural factor in appetitive virtues, to which Thomas does not even attribute the substantive beginnings of virtue. All that is naturally present is some sort of principle or structure within which virtue can develop. ("No [appetitive] habit is natural as to its beginning on the part of the soul itself, as far as the substance of the habit is concerned, but only so far as certain of its principles are concerned.") Thomas is not very explicit about what that might be, but he does suggest that it has to do with the nature of the various appetitive powers themselves, which are inclined to certain objects. In other words, we have natural appetites for particular goods—food for example—and that inclination to appetitive goods is not a function of habit but is rather the matter with which habit or virtue is concerned. Likewise, our natural knowledge of first principles of common law is undeveloped. We have a natural inclination to certain general goods, which Thomas will shortly discuss, but those inclinations are not substantive with respect to virtue. We are naturally inclined to act for the good and not for evil, which indeed can be said to be the "seed" of virtue, but *knowledge* of which goods are appropriate depends on training and experience, as do the virtues, which are habitual appetitive dispositions with respect to goods. In contrast, on the part of an individual's physical nature, Thomas then goes on to say, there are the beginnings of some appetitive virtues, but only insofar as some people are more temperamentally inclined than others "to chastity or to gentleness, or something of this kind" (I-II, q. 51, a. 1).

This does not answer the question about whether Thomas acknowledges an independent rational standard for prudence and the virtues, but it does suggest some initial difficulties with attributing to Thomas the simple notion that human nature functions as a measure of virtue. The appetitive and intellectual virtues, the habits that dispose us to authentic goods and which perfect the operation of our human powers, are natural, according to Thomas, in only a very qualified way. Nonetheless, the passage just considered does raise the question of the relationship between the virtues and naturally known first principles of practical reason, upon which most versions of natural law place so much emphasis. What Thomas has just said about first principles in general is surprisingly modest. The statement that they are naturally known is not equivalent to a claim that they are independent of experience or that they constitute some kind of innate knowledge. Rather, our knowledge of them depends on experience. The focus of Thomas's reference to first principles concerns the nature of the human subject more than the content of the principles. His point seems to be that the human species has the natural ability to apprehend and understand the world in a particular way. Once we experience what a whole is and what a part is, he says by way of example, we know that a whole is greater than a part. He does not make these observations to advance any argument about the content of first principles, and certainly not to advance any argument on the basis of first principles, but rather to make clear the limited sense in which it is accurate to say there are natural habits of the knowing powers.

Our question specifically concerns the first principles of practical reason and their relationship to prudence and the virtues. The first point to note is the difference between the principles of the practical and speculative uses of reason. Thomas repeatedly notes that the *ends* of practical reason are analogous to the *principles* of speculative reason. As a consequence, knowledge of principles is relatively more important for speculative reasoning, while appetite for good ends, the concern of the virtues, is relatively more important for reasoning about how to act. Thomas states this explicitly while refuting an objection that states prudence can be in sinners because sinners can possess the more excellent virtue of faith:

> The nature of faith consists not in conformity with the appetite for certain right actions, but in knowledge alone. On the other hand prudence implies a relation to a right appetite. *First because its principles are the ends in matters of action; and of such ends one forms a right estimate through the habits of moral virtue, which rectify the appetite:* wherefore without the moral virtues there is no prudence, as shown above [I-II, q. 58, a. 5]. (II-II, q. 47, a. 13; emphasis added)

This claim, with its stress on ends and appetite in practical reason as the functional equivalent of principles and knowledge in speculative reason, raises obvious problems for the interpretations of Thomas's ethics that stress knowledge of the first principles of practical reason or of natural law. Those interpretations tend to portray ethics as a primarily deductive science in which moral imperatives are deduced from basic naturally known moral principles. They tend to blur the distinctions Thomas makes between speculative and practical reason and to obscure his claim that the measure of speculative and practical truth is different:

The truth of the practical intellect is not the same as the truth of the speculative intellect, as Aristotle points out [*Nicomachean Ethics* IV, 2]. Truth in the speculative intellect depends on conformity of thought with the thing. And since the intellect cannot be infallibly in conformity with contingent things, but only with necessary things, hence no speculative habit about contingent things is an intellectual virtue, but only one about necessary things. Truth in the practical intellect, however, depends on conformity with right appetite. Such a conformity has no place in necessary matters, which do not come about by human will, but only in contingent matters which can originate in us, whether they be matters of interior action or products of exterior work. Hence it is solely in regard to contingent matters that we ascribe virtue to the practical intellect, art in regard to things to be made, and prudence in regard to things to be done. (I-II, q. 57, a. 6)

Apparent difficulties for my interpretation are raised, however, by the fact that Thomas sometimes talks about the importance of knowledge of universal principles of practical reason that are analogous to the universal principles of speculative reason. When he observes that in the singular matters of action with which prudence is concerned, "it is necessary for the prudent man to know both the universal principles of reason, and the singulars about which actions are concerned" (II-II, q. 47, a. 3), he is actually stressing the importance of prudence's concern with singulars against a view holding that only universal knowledge is important. Nevertheless, he does say that prudence is somehow dependent on knowledge or understanding of first principles. It is important to remember, however, that Thomas frequently argues for a middle ground between two extreme opposing positions. He is resisting the view that morality is a matter of the intellect only or the will only. We have seen his argument that the intellectual virtue of prudence depends on the moral virtues; here he is arguing that the moral virtues need intellectual virtue:

[T]here can be no moral virtue without prudence; and as a consequence there cannot be moral virtue without understanding. For it is by the virtue of understanding that we grasp the principles we come to know naturally [editor's note: That is, with little or no reasoning or discourse], in regard to both speculative and practical matters. Hence, just as right reasoning in speculative matters, insofar as it proceeds from naturally known principles, presupposes the understanding of those principles, so also does prudence, which is right reasoning about things to be done. (I–II, q. 58, a. 4)

Thomas is even more explicit about this claim in his specific discussion of prudence in *Secunda Secundae,* when he argues against the position that the end of the moral virtues is appointed by prudence (II–II, q. 47, a. 6). He states that the "ends of moral virtue must of necessity preexist in the reason" and that just as there is a natural understanding of certain things pertaining to speculative reason, "so in the practical reason, certain things preexist, as naturally known principles" (ibid.). Significantly, however, Thomas draws the important distinction I have already mentioned between the principles of speculative reason and the ends of practical reason. He says that the naturally known principles preexisting in practical reason are precisely "the ends of the moral virtues, *since the end is in practical matters what principles are in speculative matters,* as stated above [II–II, q. 23, a. 7, ad 2; I–II, q. 13, a. 3]" (ibid.; emphasis added).

Knowledge of ends is a very different matter from knowledge of principles, which is one of the reasons Thomas distinguishes between the speculative and practical employments of reason. One of the reasons for *comparing* practical and speculative understanding is to make the point that practical understanding is very much a rational activity, perfected by an intellectual virtue. The importance of the *difference,* as far as this study is concerned, is that the practical mode of reasoning perfected by prudence is dependent on virtues governing the appetite. Once again, speculative and practical reasoning depend on some kind of knowledge or apprehension of first principles. In the case of practical reasoning, however, the ends of action are equivalent to principles. Thomas says that "foremost among the things dictated by natural reason are the ends of human life, which are to the practical order what naturally known principles are to the speculative order" (II–II, q. 56, a. 1). We are correctly ordered to those ends through the virtues, and our endeavors to attain them are directed by prudence:

[P]erfection and rightness of reasoning in speculative matters depends upon the principles from which the reasoning proceeds, for, as we have said [q. 57, a. 2], science depends upon understanding, which is the habit of principles, and science presupposes such understanding. *Now in human acts, ends stand in the same relation as principles do in speculative matters. Consequently, for prudence, which is right reasoning about what is to be done, it is required that man be well disposed in regard to ends, and this depends on right appetite.* Hence for prudence, one must have moral virtue, which rectifies the appetite. (I-II, q. 57, a. 4; emphasis added)

This stress on the importance of ends as opposed to principles does not completely resolve the problem. Even if Thomas is not claiming that we have natural knowledge of principles, he still has said we have natural knowledge of ends. Prudence, he observes, is concerned with means, which are analogous to the conclusions of speculative reasoning (II-II, q. 47, a. 6). Furthermore, knowledge of ends is not obtained through the virtues, but through synderesis, which identifies the end to which the moral virtues tend. The virtues are moved by prudence, he adds, "yet *synderesis* moves prudence, just as the understanding of principles moves science" (ibid.; reply to objection 3). This appears to be confirmation of the standard view I have been trying to refute.

What is at issue here, however, is not whether Thomas ever employs the natural-law vocabulary of synderesis, first principles, and natural knowledge of ends. He obviously does. The question is what he means by that vocabulary and what he does with it. My argument at the beginning of this essay was that there is a dominant family of interpretations according to which Thomas achieved the famous synthesis of the natural law and Aristotelian moral traditions by placing the virtues in the service of substantive naturally known moral principles. So far, I have been presenting textual evidence to suggest that prudence and the virtues have priority. My task, when confronted with one of the instances in which Thomas uses the natural-law vocabulary, is to make sense of it in a way that is consistent with the interpretation I have been proposing, much as the standard natural-law interpretations have tried to accommodate Thomas's use of Artistotelian vocabulary. In short, the presence of natural-law language does not in itself count against the interpretive stress on prudence and the virtues unless it cannot be satisfactorily explained.

Thomas suggests an explanation in article 7 immediately following. Before turning to article 7, it is worth noting a claim (at II-II, q. 47, a. 6) that I shall comment on later in connection with another article. That is Thomas's statement that synderesis *moves* prudence. For now, I only wish to raise the possibility that Thomas's concern in talking about natural knowledge of first principles is not primarily with the content of the principles or the nature of the ends themselves, but rather with an explanation of the origin of prudence's deliberations. Thomas is interested in the causes of things. Synderesis serves the function of explaining how we begin to reason practically, but it does not provide content for our moral deliberations. I shall return to this point shortly.

The question Thomas addresses in article 7 is whether prudence is concerned with determining the mean of the virtues (II-II, q. 47). His argument in the affirmative sheds considerable light on our question about the meaning of Thomas's reference to naturally known ends to which the virtues tend. His initial statement recalls a preceding definition of a virtue (II-II, q. 47, a. 5, objection 1) as that which "follows a mean appointed by reason even as a wise man decides." The link between what is appointed by reason and what a wise man decides is not insignificant, because apart from the prudent deliberations of a wise individual, the notion of a mean appointed by reason is empty. Thomas begins to elaborate his response by stating that the "proper end of each moral virtue consists precisely in conformity with right reason" (ibid.). Remember that our question is what Thomas means by an end appointed by or in conformity with reason. Thomas explains that "temperance intends that man should not stray from reason for the sake of his concupiscences; fortitude, that he should not stray from the right judgment of reason through fear or daring" (ibid.). Thomas's position could hardly be stated more plainly. The naturally known end to which the virtue of temperance is inclined, for example, is the end of acting reasonably with respect to concupiscible desires. Likewise, the end to which fortitude tends is that of acting reasonably with respect to the passions of fear or daring. We have been conditioned by the standard interpretations to want a more explicit answer from Thomas, a description of an end that would tell us how to act, but the general standard of reasonableness is the one that Thomas provides.

To be sure, according to Thomas, "this end is appointed to man according to *natural reason,* since natural reason dictates to each one that he should act according to reason" (ibid.; emphasis added). What is somewhat shocking to our expectations, however, is Thomas's refusal to equate natural knowledge with specific moral knowledge that can guide conduct apart from the activity of prudence and the virtues. Thomas straightforwardly claims that "it belongs to the ruling of prudence to decide in what manner and by what means man shall obtain the mean of reason in his deeds" (ibid.). He recapitulates this answer in his reply to objection 3:

> Moral virtue after the manner of nature intends to attain the mean. Since, however, the mean as such is not found in all matters after the same manner, it follows that the inclination of nature which ever works in the same manner, does not suffice for this purpose, and so the ruling of prudence is required. (Ibid.)

It might be helpful at this point to review the argument made thus far by considering some additional passages where Thomas talks about natural virtue, natural inclinations, and natural knowledge and their relation to the deliberations of prudence. His main point about the virtues is that they are developed habits, but he acknowledges two respects in which they can be described as natural: They can be natural to the species and natural to individuals. There are two ways in which virtue is natural to the human species, he says. First, human reason possesses "certain naturally known principles," which he describes as "the seeds of intellectual and moral virtues" (I-II, q. 63, a. 1). Second, the human will has "a certain natural appetite for good in conformity with reason" (ibid.). There is also a way in which virtue can be natural to an individual, because "by certain bodily dispositions some are disposed either better or worse to certain virtues" (ibid.). In both instances, Thomas points out, the natural presence of virtue is only "incipient":

> In such manner, both intellectual and moral virtues, according to a certain incipient aptitude, are in us by nature, but not in their perfection. The reason for this is that nature is determined to one way of acting, and the fulfillment of these virtues is not brought about by one mode of acting, but by various modes, corresponding to the different matters with which the virtues are concerned and according to the various circumstances. (Ibid.)

We have already encountered this claim. That is, according to Thomas, we have a natural knowledge of certain principles of practical reason. The standard assumption is that those principles, which Thomas says are actually ends, provide concrete moral guidance and function as premises from which one can deduce specific moral imperatives in the same way that one deduces scientific conclusions from premises in speculative reasoning. As we have seen, however, when Thomas describes these first principles they convey only the general imperative that one ought to act according to reason with respect to the matter with which the virtues are concerned. The virtue of prudence determines what is reasonable in each case. Thomas's other instance of natural virtue is an individual physical predisposition. The importance of what Thomas is saying about individual predispositions does not depend on a physiology of bodily humors or some more contemporary equivalent. His emphasis in both cases is on the incipient as opposed to developed state of natural virtue. Virtue is natural in the sense that our species is created in such a way as to have an "incipient *aptitude*" for the development of the virtues. Whenever we act, we act for the sake of some good. Thomas goes so far as to say that we have a natural knowledge that we ought to act reasonably with respect to goods, but the orientation of our will to authentic goods and our deliberations about how to achieve them are entirely dependent on the virtues we are able to develop with practice over a lifetime. Prudence determines what is reasonable.

One might ask why Thomas needs to employ the natural law vocabulary of natural knowledge and inclination if it arguably does not fulfill the function commonly claimed for it. It seems, after all, that there are ways in which one could articulate a theory of the virtues quite independent of any natural-law language. Two responses to this question are particularly plausible. First, as I have already suggested, this is the obverse of the question facing the standard natural-law interpretations of Thomas's ethics: Why does a deductive system of natural law require a rich description of the virtues? A compelling response in both cases is to observe that Thomas is wrestling with two traditions: the classical Aristotelian tradition of the virtues and the Christianized Stoic and Roman tradition of natural law. I am suggesting that Thomas does succeed in achieving a synthesis, but not the synthesis ordinarily described. That is, Thomas does articulate a version of natural law, but not the deductive version most commentators attribute to him in which the virtues, if they are treated at all, play a minor supporting role. I have tried to show that Thomas gives the virtues much more systematic development and assigns to prudence a much more decisive role than ordinarily acknowledged. The natural-law vocabulary is not insignificant, but it does not play the role of guiding conduct, of determining right and wrong, or of providing the kind of foundational moral imperatives from which one can deduce specific judgments.

What role then does it play? One answer, the second response to the question I am posing, has already been suggested. Thomas is responding generally to an intellectual concern with causality. In this instance in particular, Thomas is concerned to explain what "moves" or "causes" the virtues and our practical deliberation: Prudence moves the virtues, and the natural knowledge of first principles through synderesis moves prudence (II-II, q. 47, a. 6). This concern also surfaces elsewhere in the material we are considering, for example in his discussion of the relation between intellectual and moral virtue. Thomas notes that "[r]eason, as apprehending the end, precedes desire for the end, but desire for the end precedes reason's reckoning about the choice of things which are for the sake of the end, which is the concern of prudence; just as in speculative matters, the understanding of principles is the source for reasoning syllogistically" (I-II, q. 58, a. 5; reply to objection 1).

My point is that natural law serves an explanatory function rather than the function of providing specific moral information. It explains how we come to reason practically without telling us how to reason, and it explains why we are able to act virtuously without guiding our actions. For Thomas, after all, we are creatures created in such a way as to be ordered to a final end. Thomas explains that just as we are ordered to our supernatural end through the action of God's grace, we are also ordered to an end of natural happiness or natural virtue. He says that "[t]his latter occurs in respect to two things. First in respect to reason or intellect, inasmuch as the intellect comprehends the first universal principles known to us by the natural light of the intellect, from which our reasoning proceeds in both speculative and practical matters [for example, that good should be done and evil avoided]. Second, through the rectitude of the will, which naturally tends to the good known by reason" (I-II, q. 62, a. 3). As we have seen and will observe again when we look at the "Treatise on Law," those principles contain no guidance for our conduct. In addition, the good to which the will naturally tends needs to be apprehended and then specified by a rational ability perfected by prudence if it is to be an authentic good and if it is to be pursued in the right way. Knowledge of and inclination toward specific authentic goods are not innate but have to be acquired. Whereas we might prefer to explain the origins of that knowledge and appetite in other terms, Thomas refers to the created features of our nature as a species to explain the origin of practical reasoning and virtue. His emphasis is on causation:

[T]he seeds or principles of acquired virtues preexist in us by nature. These principles are superior to the virtues acquired through them, just as the understanding of speculative principles is superior to the knowledge of conclusions acquired through them, and the natural rectitude of reason is superior to the rectitude of appetite which arises from the appetite's participation in reason, which rectitude belongs to moral virtue. Therefore human acts, insofar as they proceed from higher principles, can cause acquired human virtues. (I-II, q. 63, a. 2)

Once again, these naturally known higher principles, the ends of human action, are so general as to be empty of material content. The content, which depends on prudence and the virtues, is learned. I am arguing that what Thomas sometimes calls first universal principles of practical reason or natural law, which are known naturally, play the explanatory role I have described, while the secondary principles, which are acquired over time, guide conduct. The primary principles are known through synderesis, while the secondary principles are the concern of prudence. Thomas says as much in his response to the question of whether prudence is a natural or acquired virtue. He begins by stating that prudence is acquired: "The Philosopher says [*Nicomachean Ethics* II, 1] that intellectual virtue is both originated and fostered by teaching; it therefore demands experience and time. Now prudence is an intellectual virtue, as stated above [a. 4]. Therefore prudence is in us, not by nature, but by teaching and experience" (II-II, q. 47, a. 15).

He goes on to observe, however, that prudence, which is primarily concerned with "singular matters of action," does have a relationship to naturally known principles, which it "applies" to action (ibid.). In that sense, "as regards the knowledge of universals, the same is to be said of prudence as of speculative science, because the primary universal principles are known naturally" (ibid.). The difference between practical and speculative science, as Thomas has said in article 6 of the same question, is that the first principles of practical reason are actually the *ends* of action. As he says here in article 15, they are "connatural to man." That is, they are ends to which humans by nature are inclined. We shall look in more detail at these ends or natural inclinations in a subsequent section, but we have already seen evidence of how general and abstract they are. Thomas says repeatedly in the "Treatise on Happiness" that we are inclined by nature to the good, so that we always act for the sake of the

good. What we are lacking, however, apart from revelation, is any independent knowledge of what the good is. To be sure, the human good is to live
in accord with virtue, but only the "seeds" of virtue are naturally present.
As we have seen, what those seeds consist in, insofar as they can be
expressed as principles, is the knowledge that one should act reasonably.
As we shall see, insofar as those seeds are described as natural inclinations or naturally known ends, which are the concern of the virtues, all we
know is that one should act virtuously with respect to those inclinations.
In order to know what acting reasonably requires, and in order to act
virtuously, one is dependent on prudence.

There is another category of universal principles that Thomas calls
secondary principles. He explicitly states that these "are not inherited
from nature, but are acquired by discovery through experience, or through
teaching" (II-II, q. 47, a. 15). Without entering into the debate about
Thomas's distinctions between primary and secondary principles (see
Armstrong, 1966, and my discussion in Chapter 1), I merely suggest at this
point that we think of these secondary principles as prudential rules of
thumb, moral generalizations based on the experience of a community or of
prudent individuals, which are universal in the loose sense that they apply
most of the time. For my purposes, it is enough to point out Thomas's
observation that they are experientially rather than naturally known.

Prudence is primarily concerned with "the knowledge of particulars
which are the matter of action" (ibid.). Thomas notes that "the right ends
of human life are fixed" (ibid.), which is to say there is a general
way in which we ought to act (in accord with virtue) and that we are
created in such a way as to be ordered to certain goods. The apparent
goods we pursue, the ends for which we act, are not indifferent. Some
apparent goods are not good in reality, and in any given situation, some
authentic goods ought to be chosen over others. Thomas grants, as we
have seen previously, that some individuals have a natural inclination or
disposition to some good ends by virtue of their temperament, and in that
sense they have the natural beginnings of virtue (ibid.). Thomas elsewhere points out, however, that this kind of incipient virtue associated
with an individual's natural disposition is neither developed nor reliable:

> The natural inclination to the good of virtue is a kind of beginning
> of virtue, but is not perfect virtue. For the stronger this inclination
> is the more dangerous it could be unless it is accompanied by
> right reason, through which choice is made to a suitable end. For

example, if a running horse is blind, the faster it runs the more forcefully will it strike something and the more severely will it be injured. Consequently, although moral virtue is not right reason, as Socrates maintained, neither is it only being in accord with right reason, inasmuch as it inclines one to what is in accord with right reason, as the Platonist held, but it must also be present with right reason, as Aristotle says [*Nicomachean Ethics* VI, 13]. (I-II, q. 58, a. 4)

It is prudence, of course, that is right reason about action and that governs our choices to a right end. These choices cannot be predetermined because "the means to the end, in human concerns, far from being fixed, are of manifold variety according to the variety of persons and affairs" (ibid.). As a result, knowledge about how to choose is not natural, but must be learned. The realm of choice with which prudence is concerned, the means toward ends, extends all the way to the naturally known first principles or general ends of human nature. Because prudence is concerned with the whole range of means to our natural ends, and because "knowledge of those means cannot be in man naturally," Thomas insists that "prudence is not from nature" (ibid.).

Even the standard natural-law interpretations grant that prudence is not from nature. The real issue between my interpretation and the usual reading of Thomas's ethics has to do with the scope of prudence's deliberations and the function of first principles. I readily acknowledge that Thomas assigns an important role to the insights of synderesis or to natural knowledge of first principles. I have tried to suggest, however, that such knowledge serves the explanatory function of accounting for how it happens that we come to reason practically and for the origin of the virtues. Thomas's general point is that we have a created, natural ability to act for the good appropriate to our nature and to develop the habits that perfect that capacity. Concrete knowledge of how to act, knowledge of right means to attain the good, depends on prudence, an acquired ability, which is right reason about human action.

Knowledge of universal first principles of practical reason *is* significant insofar as it pertains to Thomas's concern about causality. That knowledge is insignificant with respect to guiding action. So far I have been substantiating this claim primarily by pointing out Thomas's predominate orientation to the virtues, his stress on the role of prudence, and his interest in explaining what "moves" practical reason and the virtues. But

Thomas also states quite explicitly that knowledge of universals is of relatively minor importance because it is unreliable and insufficient to guide actions. Right reason about action is the domain of prudence, and Thomas says that "[p]rudence consists chiefly, not in the knowledge of universals, but in applying them to action" (II-II, q. 47, a. 16). He adds that prudence is only somewhat hindered but certainly not destroyed by "forgetting the knowledge of universals" (ibid.). (I suggest that Thomas is referring here to learned, secondary universal principles, general rules of thumb that one does not necessarily need to be able to articulate in order to act prudently.) His response to the question of whether intellectual virtue can exist without moral virtue summarizes both his interest in the causal role of universal first principles, which as he describes here are abstract and general, and his reliance on virtue instead of even secondary universal principles (the conclusions of moral science) to guide action:

> Now right reasoning requires principles from which the reason-
> ing proceeds. And reasoning about particulars must proceed not
> only from universal principles but from particular principles as
> well. As to universal principles about things to be done, man is
> rightly disposed by the natural understanding of principles, whereby
> he recognizes that no evil is to be done; or again by some
> practical science. But this is not enough for right reasoning about
> particular cases. For it sometimes happens that such a universal
> principle . . . is perverted in a particular case by some passion. . . .
> Consequently, just as a man is disposed rightly with regard to
> universal principles by natural understanding or by the habit of
> science, so in order to be rightly disposed with regard to the
> particular principles concerning things to be done, which are
> ends or goals, he must be perfected by certain habits, so that it
> becomes connatural, as it were, to him to judge rightly about the
> end. This comes about through moral virtue, for the virtuous
> person judges about the end of virtue rightly. (I-II, q. 58, a. 5)

Although we have not yet considered the "Treatise on Law," most of what needs to be said about the doctrine of natural law has already been suggested in the preceding discussion of naturally known first principles and natural inclinations. Because the standard accounts of Thomas's ethics rely almost exclusively on parts of the "Treatise on Law" that discuss natural law, it will be useful to turn next to those texts.

4

NATURAL LAW

*[T]he law, as to its essence, resides in him that rules and measures;
but, by way of participation, in that which is ruled and measured;
so that every inclination or ordination which may be found in
things subject to the law, is called a law by participation. . . . And
so the law of man, which, by the Divine ordinance, is allotted to
him, according to his proper natural condition, is that he should
act in accordance with reason.*

—*Summa Theologica*

I

As we have seen, the bulk of Thomas's teaching about practical reasoning occurs elsewhere than in the "Treatise on Law," questions 90 through 108 of the *Prima Secundae* (subsequent references to the "Treatise on Law" will be to the 1947 edition of the *Summa*). Moreover, a great deal of discussion pertinent to the question about the relation between the virtue of prudence and natural law occurs in the "Treatise on the Virtues" and in the questions of the *Secunda Secundae* devoted to prudence. Focusing on the "Treatise on Law" as the primary source for understanding Thomas's ethics not only fails to attend to what he says about prudence and the virtues, making it appear that he is mainly concerned to convey an ethics of law, but also tends to distort his teaching about natural law itself. Natural law, I suggested in the preceding chapter, functions largely as a causal explanation of what "moves" practical reasoning. This might not be readily apparent to a reader of only question 94, concerning the natural law, who is unfamiliar with Thomas's previous account of practical reasoning and who presumes that natural law functions to provide guidance for action.

Nothing in the "Treatise on Law" threatens to undermine the claims I have already made about prudence and natural law. Still, it will be useful to examine Thomas's teaching about natural law in this section of the *Summa* because this is the material most often cited in support of the standard interpretations of Thomas's ethics and, as a result, the material with which readers are most familiar. I am not proposing to explicate Thomas's entire teaching about law, or even to interpret the whole of his teaching about natural law, but rather to investigate the role assigned to natural law and to make clear its relation to an ethics of prudential virtue.

II

First, a review of Thomas's understanding of law in general: Whereas Thomas presented habits or virtues as the *intrinsic* principles of human acts, he presents law and grace (grace is treated in the questions immediately following the "Treatise on Law") as the *extrinsic* principles of our acts. They are extrinsic because they depend on the action of God the Creator, Sustainer, and Redeemer of creation. The discussion of law is immediately set in the context of a theological claim about what moves us to our ultimate end: Thomas begins the "Treatise on Law" by referring the very notion of law in general to God, who is "the extrinsic principle moving to good, . . . who both instructs us by means of His Law, and assists us by His Grace" (I-II, q. 90; introduction).

Thomas describes law in general as something essentially rational. His argument for this description follows from his claim that law is something that rules and measures acts. Reason, he says, is the primary ruler and measurement of acts "since it belongs to reason to direct to the end, which is the first principle in all matters of action" (I-II, q. 90, a. 1). He then points out that there are two ways in which law can be understood as a rule and measure. According to the first way, law is something that actually rules and measures something else. This is what it means to say that law is in reason, because reason is that by which we judge human acts. According to the second way, law is a rule or measure insofar as something has an inclination in a particular direction because of some law of its nature. In this second sense, "law is in all those things that are inclined to something by reason of some law: so that any inclination arising from a law, may be called a law, not essentially but by participation as it were" (ibid.; reply to objection 1). His general definition of law is that "it is nothing else than an ordinance of reason for the common good, made by him who has care of the community, and promulgated" (I–II, q. 90, a. 4). Natural law fits the definition because it proceeds from God's reason, the eternal law, which is concerned with the common good of creation. It is promulgated, Thomas says, "by the very fact that God instilled it into man's minds so as to be known by him naturally" (ibid.).

We have already seen that Thomas portrays our participation in natural law in two ways: first, as being a matter of cognizance of first principles of practical reason analogous to the first principles of speculative reason and, second, as a matter of our inclination to the good. The two expressions of our sharing in natural law overlap. The first principle of practical reason, that good should be done and evil avoided, refers to our most basic inclination: always to act on the basis of desire for an apprehended good. We are created with both reason and appetite, according to Thomas, and we participate in the natural law both rationally and appetitively. Our knowledge of good in either mode, however, is general and abstract. The first principle of practical reason, or the first principle of natural law, does not tell us which goods in particular to pursue or how to pursue them, and our natural inclinations are only toward the general kinds of goods with which our various powers are concerned. In order to pursue appropriate goods, and in order to act reasonably with respect to our inclinations, we are dependent on the virtues under the direction of prudence, which is right reason about how to act.

Before examining Thomas's expression of these themes in the "Treatise on Law," it is worth noting that many discussions of natural law misleadingly stress the distinction between a natural moral law and the kinds of laws of nature that one would study in the natural sciences. In order to understand Thomas's use of natural law properly, it is important to see that the two understandings of law are related. To be sure, he distinguishes between the two meanings of law, but in both cases law has to do with reason, especially God's reason. The moral law of our nature, that we should act in accordance with reason, is of a piece with the created pattern or law of our nature as a species. We are created in the image of a rational God in whose reason we participate in two ways: We are unique as a species in that we have the power of reason to measure or judge our own acts, yet we also share with other species certain created inclinations, which are the laws, as it were, of our nature. Thomas's fundamental understanding of law refers to the reason of God as the principle of creation. Law in all of its manifestations derives from God's reason. Law is not first of all a juridical concept. This is even suggested in Thomas's order of presentation. He starts with the topic of law in general then moves to the different kinds of law: eternal law, natural law, and finally human law. He concludes the treatise by discussing the old and new law, the divinely revealed part of eternal law. We need to take care not to reverse the thrust of Thomas's exposition. The temptation, given the usual presuppositions about Thomas's use of natural law as the fundamental source of knowledge for guiding conduct and distinguishing good from evil acts, is to understand natural law narrowly in terms of codified human law rather than broadly in terms of God's rational plan for creation.

We have already encountered Thomas's repeated claim that God has created us in such a way as to be ordered to an end constituting our ultimate happiness and complete good. We have also encountered his claim that the happiness and good for humans, at least as far as this life is concerned, is to live in accord with virtue, and that our final and super-natural end consists in the happiness of unity with God. If we suspend the presumption that law for Thomas is primarily a juridical notion, it is possible to appreciate the sense in which these claims are the context for Thomas's understanding of natural law.

Law in all its manifestations concerns the common good, and God's eternal law concerns the good of creation, Thomas argues. Law, as the "rule and measure" of human acts, belongs essentially to reason, a "principle of human acts" (I-II, q. 90, a. 2). In practical reason, he goes on to say, the first principle or primary object is the last end, which is happiness. So law, as rational, is concerned with the various kinds of happiness constituting the common good of the human species (ibid.). He claims in the reply to objection 3 that "[j]ust as nothing stands firm with regard to the speculative reason except that which is traced back to first indemonstrable principles, so nothing stands firm with regard to practical reason unless it be directed to the last end which is the common good: *and whatever stands to reason in this sense, has the nature of law*" (ibid.; emphasis added).

The statement that whatever "stands to reason" with respect to the attainment of the last end of human life has the nature of law is significant because it underscores the breadth of Thomas's use of the concept of law in relation to practical reason. Law is tied to the two themes of reason and of inclination to an end. Whatever is reasonable concerning our last end, which from the perspective of the kind of happiness obtainable in this world consists in virtuous activity, can be described as a law. It is well to keep this model of law in mind as an alternative to the juridical and deductive model as we consider Thomas's account of natural law. When Thomas says that some act "belongs" to the natural law, he does not necessarily mean that the judgment about its rightness is a conclusion deduced from independently known first principles. To be sure, practical reasoning depends on the first principle of our nature (which can be stated as the claim that we act for the sake of the good), but moral judgments can have the status of belonging to law, in the sense that they are reasonable and tend toward the attainment of our proper happiness, without being dictates of natural law as it is ordinarily conceived.

III

When Thomas answers the question of whether there is a natural law in humans, he begins by restating his observation that law can be understood as being a rule and measure as well as being in what is ruled and measured by a law. In the latter sense, he says, the natures of all creatures participate in the eternal law because they are governed by the provident rule of God who has "imprinted on them . . . their respective inclinations to their proper acts and ends" (I-II, q. 91, a. 2). In other words, there is a natural law in all of creation because every being receives its distinctive nature from a rational God whose wisdom or plan for creation is the eternal law. As Thomas elsewhere says, God's wisdom is a kind of law in the sense that it "moves all things to their due end" (I-II, q. 93, a. 1). What he means by eternal law, he adds, "is nothing else than the type of Divine Wisdom, as directing all actions and movements" (ibid.). All of nature is subject to or participates in the eternal law because "God imprints on the whole of nature the principles of its proper actions" (ibid., a. 3).

This participation in eternal law is especially characteristic of rational creatures, who come under God's providential care "in the most excellent way" because, in addition to having certain natural inclinations, their reason allows them to participate in God's providence by being provident for themselves (I-II, q. 91, a. 2). Being created in such a way as to be ordered to an end and having the capacity to be provident (an ability closely related to prudence) is the "participation of the eternal law in the rational creature," which Thomas says "is called the natural law" (ibid.).

Thomas refers to the statement in Psalms 4:6, "The light of thy countenance, O Lord, is signed upon us," and explains that the imprint of God's light on us is "the light of natural reason, whereby we discern what is good and what is evil, which is the function of natural law" (I-II, q. 91, a. 2). This is not to say, however, that we possess the equivalent of God's knowledge of good and evil. Rather, we participate in it in the sense Thomas has already explained: by way of our inclinations and by way of an ability to reason about the rightness and wrongness of acts. Thomas is merely stating here that the function of our reason in its practical mode of directing action is to distinguish between good and bad acts, and that *capacity*, not certain knowledge, is what we share of God's reason.

Although the natural law refers to the way in which we share as rational creatures in God's eternal law, our participation in eternal reason is limited, and we have to rely on the prudential judgments of practical reason for specific conclusions about the rightness and wrongness of particular acts as well as for more general conclusions expressed in human laws about various types of acts. Thomas relies again on the analogy between speculative and practical reasoning to make this point. He suggests that human laws, which are the product of practical reason, resemble the conclusions of speculative reason, which follow from naturally known (but not innate) indemonstrable first principles. We have already seen that knowledge of first principles—for example, the principle that a whole is greater than its parts—itself depends on experience, in this case experience of what a whole is and what a part is. (Because of the way in which we are created, it is natural for us to use our powers in characteristic ways to come to know things, which is not to say we are born with that knowledge.) He points out that just as the conclusions of speculative science are not naturally known (in the sense just described) but are "acquired by the efforts of reason, so too it is from the precepts of the natural law, as from general and indemonstrable principles, that the human reason needs to proceed to the more particular determinations of certain matters" (I-II, q. 91, a. 3).

One cannot reason to conclusions in the speculative or practical sciences without supplying experientially known information that is not found in the naturally known general first principles, which themselves have an experiential component. Moreover, given the limitations of human reason, there is great potential for error in reaching conclusions. The mode of our participation in God's reason is not full, Thomas says, but imperfect. As a result, although we know some general principles of speculative reason, we do not have "proper knowledge of each single truth, such as that contained in the Divine Wisdom" (ibid.; reply to objection 1). Likewise, "on the part of practical reason, man has a natural participation of the eternal law, according to certain general principles, but not as regards the particular determinations of individual cases, which are, however, contained in the eternal law" (ibid.). In fact, our reason's practical mode of participation in God's wisdom is even more imperfect than its speculative mode of participation, because the things with which practical reason is concerned are "singular and contingent" instead of necessary. Consequently, "human laws cannot have that inerrancy that belongs to the demonstrated conclusions of the sciences. Nor is it necessary for every measure to be altogether unerring and certain, but according as it is possible in its own particular genus" (ibid.).

Human laws are necessary because of the impossibility of applying the general and abstract principles of natural law to the great diversity and contingency of human affairs (I-II, q. 95, a. 2). It is worth noting that Thomas declines to separate the notion of law governing human affairs from the notions of virtue and happiness. One of the reasons revealed divine law was necessary was to assist us in the attainment of our proper happiness on both a supernatural and natural level by providing certain knowledge of how to act. Our supernatural happiness, as we have seen, depends on living a life in charity with God, and the level of happiness that is attainable in this life, although with great difficulty and potential for error, depends on living in accord with virtue. One of the main functions of human law, according to Thomas, is to train us in virtue: Although "man has a natural aptitude for virtue," Thomas insists that "the perfection of virtue must be acquired by man by means of some sort of training" (I-II, q. 95, a. 1). He goes on to point out the difficulty of conceiving how we could manage to train ourselves, considering our inclination, especially when we are young, to various "undue pleasures," when living virtuously largely consists in ordering our desires by reason. Although some individuals are blessed by having good dispositions, good customs or habits, and good training by their parents, others "are found to be depraved, and prone to vice, and not easily amenable to words" (ibid.). The latter sort of people need to be disciplined by laws, in the sense of being instructed in right behavior as well as in the sense of being punished for wrong behavior. It was necessary for humans to frame laws so that vicious individuals might be brought to virtue or, failing that, so "at least, they might desist from evil-doing, and leave others in peace" (ibid.).

Human laws are determinations of prudence, generalizations about what is right in the majority of cases. (Remember Thomas's delineation of various species of prudence: individual, domestic, military, and regnative or political.) Just as every moral judgment that accords with right reason belongs to the natural law, so every law that is just and reasonable gains its ultimate authority from the natural law (I-II, q. 95, a. 2). Thomas says here that there are two ways in which human laws are "derived" from natural law: by way of a "conclusion from premises" and by a "determination of certain generalities." The prohibition of killing, he notes, follows as a conclusion from the principle or premise prohibiting doing harm to another, while the specification of a particular punishment for a crime follows as a determination of the general principle requiring punishment of evildoers. Derivations of the former sort receive their force from both natural and human law, while derivations of the latter sort have only the force of human law (ibid.).

This deductive model of drawing conclusions from the natural law is somewhat misleading. Not only does one need extensive practical experience to recognize legitimate exceptions to the general prohibition of killing, for example, but Thomas says in the same article, quoting Aristotle, that "in such matters, we ought to pay as much attention to the undemonstrated sayings and opinions of persons who surpass us in experience, age and prudence, as to their demonstrations" (ibid., reply to objection 4; *Nicomachean Ethics* VI, II). The objection argues that if all law is derived from natural law, it *ought* to be possible (although in reality it is not) to give a reason for every piece of human legislation since it *is* possible to give a reason for authentic derivations from natural law. Thomas replies that prudential judgments about determinations of natural law are related to the principles of natural law to the extent that "expert and prudent men ... see at once what is the best thing to decide" (ibid.).

In other words, because of their virtue and experience, some individuals are able to see at once what a good and reasonable judgment is, without engaging in an explicit process of deduction. But deduction itself, in any event, depends on moral experience for the correct understanding and application of its terms. This is a version of the claim we have already encountered, that every rational agent knows without extensive deliberation that acts such as murder and theft are wrong. Likewise, the appetite and practical reason of a truly virtuous and prudent individual has been cultivated in such a way that often such a person can almost immediately recognize the rightness or wrongness of a proposed action or, in this case, a proposed law. Given Thomas's broad understanding of natural law, this counts as natural-law reasoning, and the specific judgment counts as a derivation of natural law, because all right reasoning about action belongs to the natural law. A prudent individual's judgment that a particular act is to be done or avoided, or that a particular law is just and reasonable, is an instantiation of the first principles of natural law that good is to be pursued and evil avoided and that one should act in accordance with reason.

To reason practically, which is one aspect of our participation in eternal law, is the law of our nature because of the way in which we are created. Or, in Thomas's words, "the law of man, which by the Divine ordinance, is allotted to him, according to his proper natural condition, is that he should act in accordance with reason" (I-II, q. 91, a. 6). That does not mean that all of our practical reasoning is in accord with right reason or that when we engage in natural-law reasoning we reason infallibly. In fact Thomas states straightforwardly that *all* of our reasoning and willing, however rightly or wrongly it is exercised, is in some sense in accordance with nature because "every act of reasoning is based on principles that are known naturally, and every act of appetite in respect of the means is derived from the natural appetite in respect of the last end. Accordingly, the first direction of our acts to their end must needs be in virtue of the natural law" (I-II, q. 91, a. 2; reply to objection 2). The first principles of natural law are so general and abstract that no one can be in error about them. Everyone acts for the sake of the good, according to Thomas, in the sense that everyone acts in order to pursue an apprehended good or to avoid an apprehended evil.

Far from guiding action (except in the sense that the possibilities for acting are limited by our created nature), natural law is a way of talking about how it is that we act at all, how it is that we are able to reason about acting, and how it is that there is broad agreement about the most general moral judgments. Natural law is part of the continuum between God's reason expressed in creation and human reason expressed in the specific ordinances of a community's legislation or in customary standards of behavior. Every law, Thomas says, derives from eternal law insofar as being an expression of reason it depends on the reason of God, the prime mover of creation. Once again, we see Thomas's concern with what moves practical reason, in this case practical reason's expression in human law:

[T]he law denotes a kind of plan directing acts towards an end. Now wherever there are movers ordained to one another, the power of the second mover must needs be derived from the power of the first mover; since the second mover does not move except in so far as it is moved by the first.... Since then the eternal law is the plan of government in the Chief Governor, all the plans of government in the inferior governors must be derived from the eternal law. But these plans of inferior governors are all other laws besides the eternal law. Therefore all laws, in so far as they partake of right reason, are derived from the eternal law. (I-II, q. 93, a. 3)

The sense in which law at the lower end of this hierarchy is derived from law at the upper end of the hierarchy—human law from natural law and natural law from eternal law—is not that specific pieces of legislation are copied from one level to another or even that particular laws at one level are deductions from more general laws at a higher level. To be sure, Thomas says that practical reasoning proceeds from first principles (I-II, q. 91, a. 3), and that rational creatures participate most fully in the Divine wisdom in that they have "some knowledge of the eternal law" (I-II, q. 93, aa. 3 and 6). But the naturally known principles from which practical reasoning proceeds (which are not to be understood as innate) do not help us know what to do. The first principles of natural law are too general and abstract to guide action, and the secondary principles are experientially derived to a much greater degree, reflecting the judgments of prudence.

The standard attempt to discover which principles in particular Thomas held to be primary and which to be secondary, tertiary, and so on, and therefore more or less immediately known, is misled by its presumptions about the nature and function of natural law. If we set aside those presumptions, we can see that the authority of a moral judgment does not hang on the distinction between primary and secondary principles. That is, if moral judgments do not depend on apprehension of natural law for their content, they cannot be validated by locating them at some point in the hierarchy of natural law. In one sense, there is an infinite number of principles of natural law because all right reasoning about action belongs to the law of nature. Thomas's reference to primary and secondary principles is merely a way of saying that some moral judgments are more general and more obvious than others. Some general judgments are so obvious that they are known with little or no deliberation (although not without experience). In another sense, there is only one first principle of natural law and every other principle is secondary because every particular moral judgment is a prudential specification of the first principle stating that good is to be done and evil avoided.

Thomas makes this point repeatedly, usually in conjunction with the familiar comparison of speculative and practical reason. Just as the law of noncontradiction, the first principle of speculative reason, follows from the immediate apprehension of being, so the first principle of practical reason follows from the apprehension of good:

> Now as *being* is the first thing that falls under the apprehension simply, so *good* is the first thing that falls under the apprehension of the practical reason, which is directed to action: since every agent acts for an end under the aspect of good. Consequently the first principle in the practical reason is the one founded on the notion of good, viz., that *good is that which all things seek after.* Hence this is the first precept of law, that *good is to be done and pursued, and evil is to be avoided.* All other precepts of the natural law are based upon this: so that whatever the practical reason naturally apprehends as a man's good (or evil) belongs to the precepts of the natural law as something to be done or avoided. (I-II, q. 94, a. 2; emphasis in the original)

The basic claim is that reasoning proceeds "in various ways" from naturally known first principles (principles that are natural for us to know, but which are not innate) to specific conclusions (I-II, q. 100, a. 1). In speculative as well as practical matters, sometimes the conclusions are "so evident, that after very little consideration one is able at once to approve or disapprove of them by means of these general first principles: while some matters cannot be the subject of judgment without much consideration of the various circumstances, which all are not competent to do carefully, but only those who are wise" (ibid.). It is not always clear whether the distinction between primary and secondary precepts refers to the distinction between first principles and the conclusions that follow from them, or to the observation Thomas is making here, that some primary conclusions follow almost immediately from first principles while other secondary conclusions require more deliberation. As I have suggested, it was not crucial for Thomas to have developed this discussion with the thoroughness or consistency that later natural-law theorists would have wished because he was not providing a formula for natural-law reasoning.

However we resolve fine points in the debate about the relationship between primary and secondary principles, the most important point is that Thomas recognizes a spectrum of certainty about practical knowledge. He says that every moral judgment belongs to the natural law, but not all belong in the same way. The examples he provides of "things which the natural reason of every man, of its own accord and at once, judges to be done or not to be done" are honoring parents and the prohibitions against killing and stealing. (The Latin for the commandment commonly rendered as "Thou shalt not kill" is *Non occides*. The verb *occidere* is ambiguous because it can be translated as "to kill" or, as I shall suggest is more appropriate in this case, "to murder.") The example he gives of a moral requirement that needs to be taught by the wise is respecting elders. There are still other requirements that we would not know without divine revelation, he says, such as the prohibitions of making graven images and of taking God's name in vain (I–II, q. 100, a. 1). Although it may appear less evident in segments of our culture than in Thomas's that parents should be honored, his claim that stealing and killing (in the sense of murder) are obviously wrong is a claim that one can make without being committed to the standard version of natural law.

The issue, of course, is what one means by obvious. All Thomas means by saying that some moral judgments are reached by reason "of its own accord and at once" is what he has already said in the preceding paragraph of the response section in the same article: that "some matters connected with human actions are so evident, that *after very little consideration one is able at once to approve or disapprove of them* by means of these general first principles" from which all practical reasoning proceeds (ibid.; emphasis added). The translation of Thomas's example of the prohibitions of *occidere* (killing/murder) and *facere furtum* (stealing) is somewhat unfortunate (and complicated by traditional interpretations of the ten commandments) because the moral judgment of actions expressed by the terms, as Thomas himself employs them, is not equivalent. While stealing is already a moral term that means, at least for Thomas, unjustified taking of property belonging to someone else, the term killing does not automatically mean the unjustified taking of human life. To be sure, one needs a good reason to kill, but Thomas thinks that killing is justified in some circumstances. It is always wrong to steal, but it is sometimes permitted to kill.

Another way of putting this is to say that killing is a natural species of an act while stealing is a moral species of an act. Acts in a natural species are sometimes good and sometimes evil, depending on the circumstances (understood in Thomas's sense). Deeds in the moral species of evil acts are always wrong. There are always conceivable exceptions to prohibitions or commandments of natural species of acts because such prohibitions or commandments, sometimes described as general principles of practical reason, function as rules of thumb. To place an act in its moral species, however, its to claim that the prohibition or commandment concerning the act is exceptionless. Acts in the *natural* species of killing another person are *generally* prohibited (conceivable exceptions are killing someone as a last resort in defense of an innocent victim or killing enemy combatants in a just war), while acts in the *moral* species of murder are *always* prohibited.

When we are talking about species of acts, we are talking about general classes of acts. It is always a judgment of prudence whether a particular act should be placed in the moral species of good or evil acts. It is a judgment of prudence that some specific act of taking another's property is unjust taking and therefore an instance of theft. Thomas's point is clear if we revise the translation by substituting the word murder for killing. His simple claim is that one does not have to be trained in moral philosophy to know that stealing and murder are wrong. Although Thomas does not argue this way, we might say that one only has to know the language in which the notions of murder and stealing are expressed to know that they are wrong. It would be very peculiar, after all, for Thomas to be trying to prove the immorality of theft and murder, which is obvious as far as he is concerned. The issue is not whether they are wrong, but how we come to know that they are.

As he puts it, all practical reasoning *proceeds* from first principles. I have argued that this is an explanatory claim. Within the sphere of practical knowledge, moral judgments range from very general and obvious conclusions to very particular and difficult conclusions. One needs experience for any kind of reasoning, including the knowledge of first principles, Thomas has said. For example, one needs to have experienced what a part and a whole is in order to be cognizant of the basic speculative principle that a whole is greater than a part. Likewise, one needs some experience, but not much ability or practice in reflecting on experience, to be cognizant that theft and murder are wrong. We can "disapprove of them" after "very little consideration." Once more, context is important for a correct understanding of Thomas's position. He raises this whole issue in his affirmative answer to the question of whether the moral precepts of the "old law" are included in the natural law. He replies that *every* moral precept belongs to natural law, but then points out that a precept's inclusion in natural law does not guarantee our knowledge of it. Some moral judgments are obvious, some need to be taught to the less wise by the wise and experienced, and some require revelation in divine law (I-II, q. 100, a. 1).

Thomas's understanding of the natural law as something general and abstract is especially apparent in his discussion of divine and human law, in which he points out the inadequacy of natural law as a guide for conduct. "The precepts of the natural law are general, and require to be determined . . . by human law and divine law" (I-II, q. 99, a. 3), not by natural insight into the rightness or wrongness of specific acts. Although precepts concerning our relation to others and to God belong to the natural law "in the abstract," it is precisely "because naturally known principles are universal," and thus too general and abstract to guide conduct on particular occasions of choice, that each of the first principles of natural law "has to be determined by Divine or human law" (I-II, q. 99, a. 4). One of the several reasons Thomas gives for why a divinely revealed law concerning human acts was necessary is that human acts belong to the class of what is "contingent and particular," about which "different people form different judgments" (I-II, q. 91, a. 4). Because our happiness consists in acting virtuously, and because we lack natural knowledge of which acts are virtuous, we need God's help beyond the natural power of reason in order to attain happiness: "In order, therefore, that man may know without any doubt what he ought to do and what he ought to avoid, it was necessary for man to be directed in his proper acts by a law given by God, for it is certain that such a law cannot err" (ibid.). Human reason does not err "in the abstract" with regard "to the universal principles of natural law," but because of the limitations of human reason, and because of the impediments of sin, human reason is "obscured in the point of things to be done in detail" (I-II, q. 99, a. 2). God therefore revealed the divine law, not only to teach us things unattainable by reason yet necessary for our ultimate happiness, but also "to remove the manifold errors to which reason is liable" regarding even the things it can attain (ibid.).

IV

Despite Thomas's teaching about the abstract generality of natural law, and despite his affirmation of the necessity for the prudential determinations of human law and the revelation in divine law as guides for conduct, he nonetheless says we can reach moral judgments about some matters, after hardly any deliberation, "on the basis of first principles" (I-II, q. 100, a. 1). Our knowledge of first principles depends on a set of natural inclinations. According to Thomas, our reason naturally apprehends as good the ends to which a variety of inclinations natural to our species are oriented. The precepts of natural law accord with the inclinations to those ends. He says that we share with all things a primary inclination to preserve our very being. Second, we share with all animals an inclination to reproduce our species and to care for and educate our progeny. Third, we possess the inclination peculiar to rational creatures "to know the truth about God, and to live in society." Anything pertaining to any of these general inclinations, he says, belongs to the natural law (I-II, q. 94, a. 2).

According to the standard versions of natural law, agreement on the list of natural inclinations is crucial because the precepts vary as the inclinations do. Because there is supposed to be universal knowledge of natural law, it is somewhat embarrassing for the theory if a consensus cannot be obtained on the basic inclinations of human nature. On my reading, Thomas's position is not threatened by disagreement with his list of inclinations, because he is merely restating in slightly more detail his claim that the law of our nature is always to act for the sake of an apprehended good. Although he identifies several broad categories of good, those categories have no direct implications for specific moral judgments. He is explaining practical reason rather than providing a formula for its operation that will guarantee correct conclusions.

This is why he can state that "[a]ll the inclinations of any parts whatsoever of human nature, e.g., of the concupiscible and irascible parts, in so far as they are ruled by reason, belong to the natural law" (ibid.; reply to objection 2). This does not mean that every exercise of those inclinations automatically accords with natural law. They have to be ruled by reason. But neither is Thomas saying that nature itself provides an independent guide for discerning whether a particular inclination accords with right reason. Our inclinations—and here Thomas is talking about the concupiscible and irascible passions — require ordering by the virtues if their exercise is to be reasonable. Natural human inclinations in general, however they might be variously enumerated, belong to the law of our nature in the sense that they are ordered to various general kinds of ends naturally apprehended by humans as good: the goods associated with the preservation of an individual's being, with the propagation of the species, and with communal life, for example. In this sense, the inclinations natural to any species belong to the natural law. Humans participate in the natural law, an expression of God's reason and providence, in a special way, however, because we have the power of reason. Therefore Thomas says that as far as humans are concerned, "whatever can be ruled by reason [as can our passions and inclinations], is contained under the law of reason" (ibid.; reply to objection 3).

It should be no surprise then that Thomas answers affirmatively in the next article to the question of whether or not the natural law includes all virtuous acts (I-II, q. 94, a. 3). He does not mean that individual acts of virtue are natural in the sense that they are performed without initial effort, training, and deliberation. He acknowledges that "many things are done virtuously, to which nature does not incline at first; but which, through the inquiry of reason, have been found by men to be conducive to well-living" (ibid.). Virtuous acts are part of natural law in the sense that they are appropriate to the rational soul, just as the production of heat, to use Thomas's example, is the operation suitable to fire. Thomas says that humans share "a natural inclination to act according to reason: and this is to act according to virtue. Consequently, considered thus, all acts of virtue are prescribed by the natural law: since each one's reason naturally dictates to him to act virtuously" (ibid.). The equation between acting according to reason and acting according to virtue is significant because it makes clear Thomas's understanding that the notions of right reason about human action and of virtue are interdependent. Nature itself does not provide reason with an independent standard. Thomas is claiming that we have a natural aptitude for virtue and even a natural inclination to act virtuously or reasonably, such that we are not blank slates but have a created predisposition, not entirely destroyed by the fall, to virtue and reason. All of God's creation, of which we are a part, is good. He is not saying, however, that we have natural knowledge of how appropriately to pursue the general sorts of goods to which we are naturally inclined. That knowledge, and the related ordering of our wills, depends on training and experience. So just as all acts of virtue, being in accord with reason, are included in the natural law, all acts of vice or sin, "as being against reason, are also against nature" (ibid.; reply to objection 2).

We are now in a better position to understand what Thomas means by his claim (above) that we can come to some general moral judgments "after very little consideration . . . by means of these general first principles" (I-II, q. 100, a. 1). Given our natural inclination to the good of living in society, for example, one does not need to deliberate very long to judge that murder and theft are acts opposed to that good. Thomas is primarily interested in accounting for why we are able to make that judgment, not in defending it: We are created in such a way that our nature as a species inclines us in various directions, for example, to want to live in community. We are created in such a way that we naturally act for the sake of an apprehended good, and, more specifically, we naturally act to obtain the various kinds of goods to which our appetitive and intellectual powers are ordered. We are created in such a way that we have the ability to reflect on our inclinations and to choose the means to the good for ourselves. Some moral determinations are so obvious that particular judgments, such as the judgment that murder and theft should be prohibited, can be made almost immediately. Still, we are dependent on prudential judgment for knowledge of which acts in particular count as murder or theft.

The claim that nature provides us with inclinations to some very general kinds of goods is another way of saying that God ordered us to various goods by creating us as he did. As animals, for example, we need the good of nourishment to survive as individuals and the good of sexual reproduction to survive as a species. The inclinations to those goods are the "laws" of our nature, as they are for all animals. As rational animals, we have the ability to choose various means of obtaining those goods. Because the power of reasoning practically is part of our nature, and because we therefore participate in a special way in God's reason or eternal law, every action, power, and passion under the control of reason *especially* belongs to the natural law. It is up to practical reason perfected by prudence to decide how to act. Nature provides only the most general sort of guidance in the sense that natural inclinations provide the very wide boundaries within which prudential reason operates. In other words, according to Thomas's account of our inclinations, practical reason under the direction of prudence is concerned with obtaining physical, social, intellectual, and spiritual goods. We do not naturally know, however, how any of those goods are rightly (which is to say reasonably and virtuously) to be obtained, except in the sense that it is natural for rational creatures to reason about such matters. We do not have natural knowledge of the moral species of acts. The moral specification of acts is a prudential judgment of practical reason.

Although I take this to be Thomas's general position, he is not entirely consistent. Sometimes, especially when he is discussing sexual sins, he slips into a crude kind of physical naturalism. In other words, Thomas's predominant emphasis when discussing natural law is on what is in accord with reason (however that is interpreted), but sometimes he refers moral judgment about sexual behavior directly to observations about what "is natural to all animals." Thus he says that a sin against nature can be *either* a sin against reason *or* a sin against "that nature which is common to man and other animals; and in this sense, certain special sins are said to be against nature; thus contrary to sexual intercourse, which is natural to all animals, is unisexual lust, which has received the special name of the unnatural crime" (I-II, q. 94, a. 3; reply to objection 2).

There are several possible interpretations of Thomas's argument in this passage. One option is to read it as a clear example of Thomas's understanding of natural law. On this reading, Thomas is concerned to demonstrate the sinfulness of homosexuality. His proof is the claim about its opposition to animal nature and thus to natural law. The major difficulty with this understanding of the passage is that it is at odds with Thomas's mode of argument elsewhere in the *Summa,* including his presentation of natural law in the "Treatise on Law." In fact, some proponents of the standard reading of Thomas's doctrine of natural law find this treatment of sexual sin uncharacteristic of all but Thomas's very early work (see Armstrong 1966). Using this passage as a proof text for Thomas's use of natural law thus pays the price of having to explain Thomas's alternative treatments of natural law almost everywhere else.

Another alternative is to acknowledge the idiosyncrasy of this passage and attempt to explain it from the perspective of one's interpretation of Thomas's usual treatment of natural law. This option is open to someone who accepts my interpretation of Thomas as well as to someone who holds to the standard account. One plausible explanation for why Thomas departs here from his usual mode of argument is that he formulated his position on homosexuality early in his career and never got around to revising it to cohere with his mature doctrine of natural law. Another reasonable explanation is that the act of "unisexual lust" appeared to him so strikingly wrong that it seemed entirely plausible to see its sinfulness written in the very nature of things, even though Thomas elsewhere avoids using a rational creature's animal nature as a proof for moral judgments. In other words, when something seems obviously wrong, we assume its wrongness without much thought for the reasons we give. On closer examination those reasons may need revision to cohere with reasons we give in support of other judgments.

A third option for understanding this passage is to see natural law functioning as an explanation rather than a proof. Perhaps Thomas perceived apparent disgust at homosexuality as a significant aspect of moral experience that needed explanation. The reason for experiencing such revulsion at unisexual lust, Thomas might be suggesting, is that it is contrary to our animal nature. On this reading, Thomas would not be concerned to demonstrate the wrongfulness of homosexuality, which is unquestioned from his perspective. If that were his concern, however, he presumably would proceed to discuss what he believed to be its unreasonableness and its opposition to virtue.

Of the three alternatives, I am inclined to accept the second, which treats the passage as an exception to Thomas's usual style of argument. This reading has to assume the cost of charging Thomas with an inconsistency, but the cost also has to be assumed by all but the physicalist interpretations of Thomas's natural-law teaching. There is not enough textual evidence to support the third reading, although it would complement my general interpretation and has the advantage of making Thomas consistent in his discussion of natural law. The first reading, which treats the passage as illustrative of Thomas's teaching, is opposed by too much countervailing evidence to be plausible. Rather than reading right and wrong from the physical nature shared by all animals, it is much more common, and more consistent with the entirety of his teaching about moral understanding, for Thomas to say that "since human morals depend on their relation to reason, which is the proper principle of human acts, those morals are called good which accord with reason, and those are called bad which are discordant from reason" (I-II, q. 100, a. 1).

If Thomas were teaching that we have innate knowledge of even the most general moral judgments, or that we were able straightforwardly to deduce moral judgments from naturally knowable first principles based on our natural inclinations, it would be difficult to make sense of some of his statements about the way in which everyone, including the sinner, participates in the natural law. If everyone knows a set of foundational principles about morality, failure to know how to act in a particular case can only be explained by the inadequacy of one's ability to reason syllogistically, while failure to desire to act in the right way must be explained by a lack of motivation. Such a reading trivializes or ignores Thomas's detailed account of practical reasoning and his rich description of the virtues, especially prudence.

Thomas says that the general precepts of natural law, which is "one and the same for all," are shared by the "perfect and imperfect" (I-II, q. 91, a. 5). This does not mean that the natural law is constituted by a set of basic moral judgments that apply and are equally apparent to saints as well as sinners. Thomas is arguing in this passage that there is a way in which we know the eternal law by participating in the natural law. Every-one shares a created nature reflecting Divine reason, and everyone always acts for the sake of an apprehended good. Only God knows the eternal law as it is in reality, but every rational creature shares "in its reflection, greater or less" (I-II, q. 93, a. 2) via the natural law.

As we have seen, every moral judgment that accords with reason and virtue is included in the natural law and thus in the eternal law. Further-more, according to Thomas, there are some general judgments that every rational person makes. He states that "all men know the truth to a certain extent, at least as to the common principles of natural law" (ibid.). Everyone whose reason is intact knows that the objects of our natural inclinations — food, water, reproducing the species, living in society, etc. — are good, which is not to say, of course, that there are never good reasons to refrain from pursuing these goods, or that the appropriate ways to pursue these goods is naturally apparent. Knowledge of how rea-sonably and virtuously to pursue goods is prudential. Thomas also is saying that it is obvious to every rational person that some general categories of acts are opposed to those goods. Whether particular acts belong to those categories, however, is likewise a judgment of prudence.

Every rational creature is subject to the natural law, Thomas says, but being subject means something other than being judged by a set of moral precepts built in to our reason. Along with irrational creatures we are subject "by way of action and passion," and as rational creatures we are subject "by way of knowledge" and by way of a natural inclination or adaptation " 'to be the recipients of virtue' " (I-II, q. 93, a. 6). We have already explored some of what Thomas means by these claims. In this passage he adds the observation that participation in natural law is "imperfect, and to a certain extent destroyed in the wicked; because in them the natural inclination to virtue is corrupted by vicious habits, and, moreover, the natural knowledge of good is darkened by passions and habits of sin" (ibid.). Nonetheless, even under the conditions of sin, in which one is directed by the "prudence of the flesh," there still remains enough good in one's nature so that one retains "the inclination to act in accordance with the eternal law" (ibid.). As Thomas says in the next question, the first principles of natural law, which are general and abstract, "can nowise be blotted out from men's hearts" by sin, passions, or evil customs and habits (I-II, q. 94, a. 6). What is obscured by sin are the secondary precepts, "the law of nature in particular cases" (ibid.). If everyone, including the worst sinner, participates in and has some knowledge of natural law, and if even a vicious individual possesses an *inclination* to act in accord with eternal law, of which natural law is a part, then it seems likely that natural law is something other than the set of foundational moral principles described in the standard accounts.

One of the problems faced by the standard accounts is, if natural law is known by all, as Thomas says it is, how is moral disagreement to be explained? Are cultures and communities that subscribe to a set of norms other than the set held by Thomas and his disciples guilty of moral perversity and irrationality? Not if Thomas's use of natural law is properly understood. He affirms that "all nations" have the "general principles" of the natural law in common, but he leaves room for legitimate disagreement about its details (I-II, q. 94, a. 4). As he says in the next question, "The general principles of the natural law cannot be applied to all men in the same way on account of the great variety of human affairs: and hence arises the diversity of positive laws among various people" (I-II, q. 95, a. 2; reply to objection 3).

This uncertainty about conclusions is another respect in which practical and speculative reasoning differ. In speculative reasoning, which concerns necessary things, not only the universal principles but also the conclusions hold true for all, although the truth about the conclusions is not known by everyone. In practical reasoning, which deals "with contingent matters, about which human actions are concerned," only the general first principles are universally applicable. The example of a universally true first principle, which Thomas cites three different ways in the same article, is that "it is universally right for all men, that all their inclinations should be directed according to reason" (I-II, q. 94, a. 4; reply to objection 3). The truth of a principle of this sort, Thomas says, is both universally applicable and universally known. But both the truth and the appearance of the truth of the conclusions that follow from it vary:

"[I]n matters of action, truth or practical rectitude is not the same for all, as to matters of detail, but only as to general principles: and where there is the same rectitude in matters of detail, it is not equally known to all" (ibid.).

He says that it follows from the principle that "it is right and true for all to act according to reason" (ibid.) that property entrusted to someone should be returned to the original owner, although this conclusion from a first principle of natural law is neither universally true nor universally acknowledged even when it is true. Sometimes, Thomas points out, the return of property would be unreasonable, harmful to the common good, and wrong, such as when the property would be used for treasonable purposes. He adds that the generally true principle about returning property to its rightful owner "will be found to fail the more, according as we descend further into detail" (ibid.). Conceived as a set of principles, natural law is universally true or the same for all because the principles are so general, but it differs in its details, which are the concern of prudence. It is *always* right to pursue good and avoid evil, and it is always right to act according to reason. These are the examples Thomas gives of the first principles of natural law, which are universally true and acknowledged by all. As our generalizations about action become more specific, they become less evident and less certain. It is *usually* right, because it is usually reasonable and virtuous, to repay debts or to return property entrusted to us, but sometimes circumstances arise in which it is prudent, which is to say it is right, to do otherwise.

Natural law conceived as a pattern of inclinations is also the same for all because the inclinations are likewise general. As we have seen, Thomas teaches that humans share a tendency to be oriented to the good such that we always act for the sake of an apprehended good. There are, however, some general categories of *authentic* goods to which we are naturally inclined because of the way in which we are created. Because creation itself is good rather than evil or indifferent, and because the goodness of our created nature persists even after the fall, it would be peculiar if we were not attracted to some of the good things God has made. In fact, it is surprising that Thomas declines to be more specific in his claims about our natural inclinations. All he says, though, is that along with all creatures we naturally tend to the good of preserving our being, and that along with all animals we naturally tend to the good of reproducing our species. As rational creatures, we also tend to the good of living in society, using our intellects, and knowing God.

In other words, the natural law, as understood by Thomas (most of the time), is merely a way of stating that we are created in such a way that we naturally tend to physical, social, intellectual, and spiritual goods or ends. Although Thomas has theological reasons for his claim about natural inclinations, and although it serves his purpose of explaining what moves practical reasoning, it hardly requires construal as the outlines of the version of natural law ordinarily attributed to him. I might choose a different vocabulary to explain the origins of some observed patterns of human desire, and my list of observed inclinations might be somewhat different, but I can certainly observe that it is in some sense natural for a person to want to live, eat, drink, procreate, live with others, think, and to be religious without committing myself to a full-fledged theory of natural law, especially if I refrain from using that general observation as a justification for moral judgments. I might use my observation about the general pattern of human inclination as a rough-and-ready guide for discerning whether a particular individual is rational or physically and psychologically healthy or not, so that I would look for good reasons to explain the abnormal behavior of someone who did not desire food or companionship, for example, but I am not thereby required to use that observation as a basis for judging the morality of various acts of declining food or companionship.

Thomas's teaching about natural law coheres rather than conflicts with his full-fledged ethics of prudential virtue because only his treatment of the virtues purports to be an account of how to achieve moral understanding and to make appropriate moral choices. In order to determine the rightness or wrongness of acts, according to Thomas, we have to determine whether or not they are reasonable and virtuous. That determination does not depend for its content on an apprehension of the general first principles of natural law or of practical reason, which specify the extrinsic conditions of its possibility, but on a learned habit of making such determinations well. That habit is the virtue of prudence, which, in conjunction with the other cardinal virtues attained by habituation and experience, perfects our capacity to reason practically and to judge acts in terms of their reasonableness considering their circumstances and in light of their accord with virtue.

5

THE IMPLICATIONS
FOR MODERN ETHICS

I

This essay began with observations about the impasse characteristic of modern ethics and with a claim about the relevance of Thomas's account of the virtue of prudence to contemporary attempts to extricate ourselves from what Alasdair MacIntyre has called our "modern moral dilemma." I agreed with those who propose that the classical understanding of the virtues offers the possibility of providing a useful alternative to the inadequacy of much contemporary thinking about morality, a vocabulary for dealing more productively with specific moral problems, and an account of the moral life that attends to the importance of the relation between character and community.

My focus on prudence is an attempt to increase the usefulness, interest, and rigor of the developing conversation about virtue. In order to reappropriate something like Saint Thomas Aquinas's understanding of an ethics of virtue, we need to rediscover the roles of the particular virtues. In order properly to understand the roles of and relations among those virtues, we especially need to reexamine the cardinal virtue of prudence, which in its impoverished modern guise bears an extremely remote and sometimes even hostile relation to its original role of rectifying reason about human action.

Using Thomas as a resource for enriching our understanding of the virtues and of prudence in particular raised immediate questions about how to interpret Thomas's ethics because Thomas is almost always portrayed as the great teacher of natural law. Much of this essay has been devoted to making credible the claim that we have inherited a misleading portrait of Thomas. I have tried to substantiate that proposition by providing a plausible alternative rendering: Thomas is not primarily concerned with teaching a doctrine of natural law but with presenting an account of moral understanding in which the cardinal virtues under the direction of prudence have priority.

Although this proposal for revising our understanding of Thomas's ethics flies in the face of a long and rich tradition of scholarship, it is not entirely idiosyncratic: Josef Pieper, Karl Rahner, and John Finnis are prominent among the interpreters of Thomas who consider the standard natural-law interpretation inadequate, despite profound differences among their own interpretations. Perhaps what has been lacking in the standard interpretation is perspective. What I am suggesting is that the established interpretation has been constrained by Thomas's long established and only recently diminished authority in theology and ethics. It is not implausible to suppose that once Thomas's teaching, for whatever reasons, became identified with the deductive version of natural law—so conveniently formulable for use in the confessional, for summary in manuals, and for grounding the Church's moral teaching—it became exceedingly difficult for his disciples to see him in any other light.

Thomas's teaching about the virtues has not been completely ignored or forgotten by his followers, but it has been almost completely overshadowed by the natural-law doctrine to which it was so thoroughly assimilated. Although an adequate history of the eclipse of the Aristotelian and Thomistic virtue tradition has yet to be written, it is not unlikely that the virtues and especially prudence suffered some degree of guilt by association with the Aristotelian science and Thomistic moral theology rejected in the early modern period of our history. That is, when Aristotle and Thomas became intellectual villains rather than heroes, we discarded more than the bath water when we threw out Aristotle's authority in science and Thomas's purported doctrine of natural law.

However we should most accurately tell the important story of how the virtues all but vanished from our moral vocabulary, one of the significant implications of this study about the role prudence plays in Thomas's moral teaching is that Thomas should once again be seen as a figure worthy of study for more than antiquarian reasons—at least by those interested in reviving an ethics of virtue as an alternative to modern moral theory and by those concerned to defend modern ethics against that challenge. Because modern moral philosophy considers natural law to have been refuted, especially in its religious articulations, many moral philosophers see the Thomas who is its most prominent proponent as having only historical interest. If I have successfully made the case for distinguishing between the Thomas who is associated with the natural-law doctrine and the relatively unfamiliar Thomas who is the teacher of virtue and the proponent of prudence, then the latter Thomas has immediate relevance to the contemporary debate about virtue. No one has provided a more detailed account of the role played in moral understanding by prudence, and of its relation to the other cardinal virtues of temperance, fortitude, and justice, than Thomas. If we want to rehabilitate those virtues for contemporary use, Thomas should be our teacher. Likewise, if one wants to propose an alternative account or catalogue of the virtues, or to charge that the classical conception of the cardinal virtues is incoherent or otherwise unsuited to contemporary needs, Thomas's account requires a critique.

It may be, however, that my interpretation of Thomas is mistaken, or at least that I have failed to convince my readers of the central role played by prudence and the virtues in his ethics. It may be that Thomas should remain the patron saint of the natural lawyers, or at least that there is a profound and unresolvable tension between the detailed ethics of virtue that occupies so much of the second part of the *Summa* and the comparatively brief remarks about natural law that have occupied so much scholarly attention. Even if that were so, it would remain the case that an ethics of virtue centered on prudence provides an alternative to a theory of natural law and to its modern successors, whether or not I am correct in my description of Thomas's synthesis of virtue with natural law. In short, although one of the implications of this study is that the history of ethics needs to be retold in a way that portrays Thomas as someone other than the authoritative teacher of a historically significant but now unsupportable and unfashionable doctrine of natural law, other implications of the importance of prudence and the virtues remain whether or not my interpretation of Thomas is convincing. The following discussion of some of those implications is meant to be suggestive rather than exhaustive. An attempt at a complete discussion would require reviewing the entire debate over reviving an ethics of virtue.

II

We lack wide agreement on what constitute the relevant features of an ethics of virtue, but an ethics of prudential virtue of the sort I have attributed to Thomas provides a way around the standoff between the heirs of Kantianism and consequentialism, the dominant successors to standard Thomistic natural law. To be sure, this is a drastic telescoping of a complex story, and it fails to acknowledge significant alternatives to these general ways of conceiving morality. Nonetheless, when a theologically informed understanding of natural law ceased to provide our culture's common moral (and political) vocabulary, the search for acceptable replacements eventually led in what became two main and competing directions. One of those directions, which I associate with Kant, especially in the *Groundwork of the Metaphysics of Morals,* is characterized by the attempt to establish morality through the supposed requirements of autonomous practical reason. The other direction, which I associate with consequentialism, is characterized by the attempt to make the attainment of desired outcomes the basis of morality. A shorthand but nonetheless intelligible way of conceiving modern ethics is as an accretion of increasingly sophisticated variations on these two themes formulated in response to each's criticisms of the other. Despite progress in the sophistication of the respective arguments, the two positions are balanced in such a way that the strengths and weaknesses on each side of the debate continue to be cancelled by the strengths and weaknesses of the other side, so that the argument appears to be interminable.

Consider a simple version of one set of telling criticisms generated from the perspective of a theoretical strength on one side and directed at a perceived corresponding weakness on the other: Among the most attractive features of the theories indebted to Kantianism is their ability to proclaim absolute moral judgments. One important reason for why this feature is attractive is that the ability to proclaim, for example, that theft is always wrong resonates strongly with still viable vestiges of traditional morality. This strong point is related to one of the standard criticisms of consequentialism: According to the consequentialists, if doing some ordinarily illicit act (or contravening some standard moral prohibition) would, in a specific set of circumstances, bring about a more desirable set of outcomes than not doing the act or not breaking the rule, then in that case one should do what we ordinarily think of as immoral.

The charge is simply that a consequentialist theory sometimes requires its proponents to approve actions that seem intuitively wrong. Consequentialism does too much violence to our intuitions.

On the other hand, one of the great attractions of consequentialism is its suspension of moral judgment until the relevant circumstances of the case have been considered and weighed. For the consequentialist, it is not enough to know what the act in question is but one also needs to know the context and outcome of the act before a judgment is possible. This feature also resonates with a strong and common intuition. It corresponds to one of consequentialism's most telling criticisms of theories indebted to Kantianism: the abstraction on the part of the Kantian theories from the concrete reality of the moral situation into a realm of putatively universal and timeless moral rules, which themselves occasionally require actions opposed to common intuitions. Should one never tell a lie, for example, even when the Nazi on one's doorstep asks about the location of the Jewish children hidden in the basement? The response by both sides to this sort of appeal to a pre-theoretical moral sense is frequently, "So much the worse for the intuitions."

This is, of course, a rather crude and selective characterization of what has become a series of highly refined modifications and critiques of the competing theories. The point of the portrayal is to illustrate something of the nature of the standoff between two dominant ways of thinking about morality. Each side can diagnose the other's ills, but each has been incapable of more than temporarily relieving the symptoms of its own distress.

I am not at all suggesting that virtue theory, in contrast, can succeed in silencing argument or even that such an objective would be desirable. However, an ethics of virtue does avoid the standoff over these and other characteristic problems encountered by the dominant moral theories. (For discussions of this theme, see Stanley Hauerwas, 1974, and MacIntyre, 1981.) In Thomas's explication of the virtues, as we have seen, there are moral absolutes: Vicious acts are always wrong, and one is always obliged to act in accord with virtue. At the same time, as we have also seen, one can not specify in advance of a prudential assessment of the circumstances what the requirements of virtue are. To be sure, certain generalizations can be made, and we can ordinarily rely on "rules of thumb" expressed as moral precepts. Acts that fall under the moral species of murder, theft, rape, and lying are always prohibited. Our "thou-shalt-nots" regarding them always hold. The question is not whether lying, for example, is wrong. Our sometimes painfully and slowly accumulated moral experience permits us to make that general judgment with confidence. The difficult and interesting question, to use the same example, is what counts as lying. For the making of that determination we are dependent on the judgment of prudence about a particular case, taking into account the relevant circumstances of the situation and relying on the moral insight of virtuous members of our community.

By offering alternative answers to this kind of question, such as that lying consists in the offense against justice of withholding the truth from whom it is due, an ethics of virtue creates an opening in moral conversation for the consideration of other, possibly more important questions: What circumstances of situations should be considered relevant to the moral judgment of acts? What is the nature of the relation between an agent's acts and character? In what ways are an individual's character and moral understanding dependent on the moral character of the larger community? How can virtues be cultivated in an environment where there is little consensus on the good? How should moral education be conducted? Certainly there are other accounts of moral experience challenging the dominant theories, offering their own responses to the standard set of repeatedly debated problems, and proposing their own sets of alternative concerns. An ethics of virtue is no different from these other contenders for room in the conversation in having to make a convincing case that it has something interesting, useful, and defensible to contribute. What might distinguish it from the other contenders is its continuity with our culture's moral history, its grounding in experience, and its coherence with the best of our inherited moral notions.

These observations apply to modern religious as well as secular ethics, although the movement of religious moral thinking in the general directions just described has perhaps been slower. Despite its misfortunes in the world of secular moral philosophy, the doctrine of natural law remains viable for many Roman Catholics, if not in its traditional articulation then at least in one of the modern reformulations put forward in response to modern philosophical critiques. One of the implications of a successful recovery of an ethics of prudential virtue is that it provides an attractive alternative, continuous with Catholic teaching, to the whole range of unsatisfactory natural-law options, on the one hand, and the equally unsatisfactory secular replacements. A Catholic who appreciates the force of criticisms of natural law, but who wants to use a moral vocabulary in continuity with church teaching and tradition, need not choose between defending some revisionist version of the claim that universal moral laws are written in human nature by the creator or adopting some version of consequentialism with a Christian veneer.

Versions of natural law and consequentialism are not the only moral-theoretical options available in a Roman Catholic context, but in their various manifestations they have recently been the main choices. If one accepts the rough generalization that most of modern ethics, with significant exceptions, has tended to argue either that we should obey a Kantian law of reason or that we should maximize some desired set of consequences, one can see the same options mirrored in or at least influencing Catholic ethics. The Kantian strain of moral thought has found expression in reformulations of natural law (Finnis, Anthony Battaglia, and Rahner, for example), while the consequentialist strain is expressed in situationalism or more recent proposals, such as Richard McCormick's, to maximize the proportion of pre-moral goods over evils.

McCormick resists the charge that his account of ethics is consequentialist, at least in the sense of being utilitarian. (The most important source for McCormick's theory of proportionate reason is his 1973 Marquette Lecture, "Ambiguity in Moral Choice," which appears along with responses and McCormick's reply containing revisions, "A Commentary on the Commentaries," in *Doing Evil to Achieve Good,* 1978.) Much of a more recent article by Sanford Levy, "Richard McCormick and Proportionate Reason," is devoted to explaining McCormick's reasons for denying "that proportionate reason is merely quantitative or consequentialist, and that long-run consequences 'constitute' the wrongness of acts" (1985: 266). Nonetheless, Levy argues that McCormick "could well be caught in a contradiction when he says that consequences only reveal but do not constitute or determine wrongness" (269).

According to Levy's summary, one "general sense of 'proportionate reason' . . . is the view that acts producing nonmoral evil [such as pain or death] can sometimes be right." What McCormick attempts to do is to provide a " 'structure of moral reasoning' " for balancing conflicting values "when there is proportionate reason for performing an act involving nonmoral evil" (259). The issue, of course, is not whether it is ever permissible to produce nonmoral evil. Everyone agrees that in the absence of extraordinary circumstances the pain of tooth extraction, for example, is legitimately inflicted in order to relieve the suffering produced by an impacted molar. McCormick is after a set of considerations that will distinguish that kind of act from the act of a Nazi dentist pulling teeth in order to satisfy his curiosity about how children react to pain, a set of reasons for why there is proportionate reason for doing the first act but not the second. Levy provides a good summary description of those reasons:

> In sum, McCormick believes that it is wrong to do evil to achieve good if there is no proportionate reason for the evil, and that there is no proportionate reason when the evil means undermine (or are not in the best service of) the kind of value being sought, where, in the cases McCormick is concerned with, the undermining takes place via the undermining of associated goods. This undermining effect occurs when the evil means are not necessary for the attainment of the good, and one significant kind of case in which the evil means are not necessary is when they are designed to attain the good by influencing a free and rational agent to refrain from evil. (262–63)

In the development of these kinds of reasons, which I only note here but which are elucidated in detail by Levy, McCormick seems to be trying to avoid the limitations of natural-law reasoning while also avoiding the pitfalls of consequentialism. He may have succeeded in the first endeavor, but Levy argues convincingly that the connections with consequentialist reasoning remain. If one perceives the force of the criticisms that consequentialists and Kantians have made of each other, and if one recognizes each side's ability to explain the weaknesses of the other's position and notes each's inability to account for the other's strengths, then the Christianized cousins of the secular moral theories, such as the proportionalism that is currently so popular in Catholic moral thought, are likely to appear similarly unappealing.

Although this is not the occasion to go into more detail about the problems with proportionalism, which sometimes claims inspiration from Thomas, I would like to suggest that my description of Thomas's ethics, according to which acting in accord with reason means acting virtuously, calls the proportionalists' account into question. Thomas teaches that one is obliged to act virtuously even if the consequence upsets the desired proportion of so-called pre-moral goods to evils. Like Karl Rahner, the proportionalists are right in resisting natural law's monopoly on Thomas and in challenging natural law's adequacy as an account of moral experience. But proportionalism shares a vulnerability to criticisms of consequentialism, and its account of moral reasoning is significantly different from Thomas's teaching.

III

Karl Rahner's treatment of natural law and his proposal for a "formal existential ethics" is indebted to the Kantian strain of moral reasoning as well as to some more recent influences. His ethics can be seen as an attempt to use an influential strain of modern philosophy to make natural law intellectually acceptable, to respond positively to the situationalist critique that an ethics of law fails to attend to unique persons and circumstances, and yet to use natural law to resist the tendency of all versions of consequentialism, when pushed, to legitimate acts that violate established norms. Rahner also claims that his ethics is genuinely Thomistic (see Daniel M. Nelson, 1987, for a critique of Rahner's existential ethics and for a listing of relevant sources).

If my claims about the role of prudence and the virtues in Thomas's ethics are correct, then Rahner is right in claiming that Thomas should not be associated with the version of natural law commonly attributed to him. Rahner is largely in agreement with the Thomas I have described in resisting articulations of natural law that deduce absolute and universal moral precepts, supposedly sufficient to guide human conduct, from a set of empirically observable essential elements of human nature. Where he departs from Thomas is in his use of a distinction between observable aspects of human nature that are historically, culturally, and biologically contingent (and thus inadequate as a foundation for universal norms), and a "transcendentally knowable" permanent core of human nature characterized by subjectivity and freedom (and thus also inadequate as a basis for specifying absolute moral obligations and prohibitions). The distinction not only owes more to Kantian notions of subjectivity than to Thomas's teaching, but Rahner also puts it to a use that both ignores and conflicts with what Thomas says about prudence. Rahner uses the distinction to point to the need for something other than "essential" or natural-law ethics to guide conduct, acknowledges Thomas's emphasis on prudence as a signal that Thomas recognized that some other source of moral understanding is necessary, and then proceeds to develop his account of "existential" ethics in the spirit of St. Thomas without attending to what Thomas says about prudence.

Whether or not I am right in my unorthodox reading of Thomas's treatment of natural law and in my interpretation of how that treatment coheres with his teaching about prudence and the virtues, the fact remains that Thomas has indeed provided us with a very rich account of prudential virtue. In many ways, that account satisfactorily accomplishes what Rahner attempts to accomplish with his account of existential ethics. Most generally, an ethics of prudential virtue preserves what Rahner saw as the large element of truth in situation ethics but missing in any ethics based on natural law: that there is more to individual moral obligation than can be expressed by general rules. More specifically, the three considerations that Rahner says compelled him to develop his account of existential ethics already receive ample attention in prudential ethics.

The first consideration Rahner notes is that even a reformulated version of essential ethics, one that reflects the "openness" of human essence, cannot provide a set of moral norms that adequately attend to the characteristic human freedom for spiritual and moral self-creation. Rahner does not describe that freedom in terms of autonomy but rather in terms of an obligation to love God and neighbor in ways that cannot be specified in advance by natural-law precepts. Without accepting Rahner's claims about what constitutes human essence and how it is knowable, and in particular without making freedom a metaphysical attribute knowable by transcendental reflection, one can appreciate Rahner's insight into the inadequacy of an ethics of law to encompass the sphere of moral obligation. Moral precepts concern commanded and prohibited acts, but they only indirectly concern the characters of those who do the actions. A virtue ethics, on the other hand, is concerned with an individual's obligation to be a certain kind of person as well as with the acts appropriate to a certain kind of character. As Rahner recognized, an ethics of law does not provide a vocabulary for describing or guiding the process of moral development. An ethics of virtue, on the other hand, does, and by focusing on character does so precisely. This is a point that Stanley Hauerwas makes repeatedly:

> To emphasize the idea of character is to recognize that our actions are also acts of self-determination; in them we not only reaffirm what we have been but also determine what we will be in

the future. By our actions we not only shape a particular situation, we also form ourselves to meet future situations in a particular way. Thus the concept of character implies that moral goodness is primarily a prediction of persons and not acts, and that this goodness of persons is not automatic but must be acquired and cultivated. (1974: 49)

The failure of essential or natural-law ethics to do justice to the singular reality of concrete situations is the second consideration that Rahner says compelled him to develop a supplement. Legal language has to treat situations as cases falling under general rules, which distorts their distinctiveness, Rahner observes. The imperative or prohibition governing the case never quite fits the unique features of a particular situation. He argues that the qualitatively different "pointing gesture" of existential ethics specifies without distortion exactly what one should do. Rahner is mistaken, however, in thinking that gestures, however metaphorically understood, escape the generalities of language. Language is communication and understanding, not speech alone, and gestures are not relevantly distinct from words. Nonetheless, Rahner's point about the generalities of legal language remains valid. The moral significance of a particular situation cannot be adequately understood by viewing it as merely one of a general class of cases falling under a legal precept commanding or prohibiting some kind of action. Rahner developed existential ethics as an alternative that would avoid a legal vocabulary's tendency either to prohibit too much or permit too little, and that would also avoid the opposite tendency of even a Christianized situation ethics to prohibit too little and to permit too much.

Although these options dominated the conversation in which Rahner was participating, they are not the only alternatives available in the Christian tradition. An ethics of virtue, a more attractive alternative, escapes the constraints of legal language because what it requires is virtuous character and action and what it prohibits is viciousness—obligations and prohibitions not encapsulable in a set of rules. For even when general rules function as a shorthand compendium of the prior determinations of prudence that serves both to summarize a community's accumulated moral experience and guide the untrained conscience, the demands of virtue in a particular situation cannot be specified in advance of a description of the circumstances relevant to that situation. The prudent individual, however, is a virtuoso in discerning and weighing the morally relevant features or circumstances of situations and then acting appropriately.

An ethics of virtue simultaneously avoids the antinomian tendencies of situation ethics because the tradition of the virtues provides a vocabulary for giving a much richer account of what it does and does not mean to do the virtuous thing in a given situation than is given, for example, by Joseph Fletcher's account (1966) of what it means to do the loving thing. When we talk about what it means to be virtuous in terms of Thomas's description, we are not talking about being good or doing the right thing in some vague way that leaves all the further specification up to the autonomous discretion and impulse of each individual, but we are talking about being prudent, temperate, brave, and just in a way that can be publicly defended and challenged by referring to a community's inherited understanding of the meaning of those dispositions and of the characteristic kinds of behavior they prompt.

The third factor that Rahner mentions as compelling existential ethics is the fact that the negative and positive precepts of a natural-law ethics lay out only the boundaries of moral action. Rahner acknowledges that the prohibitions of natural law cannot be contradicted, but he observes that its commandments are so broad that the individual is left facing a variety of permitted options without guidance. These choices are not morally indifferent — some permitted options are better than others — but an ethics of natural law has little if anything to say about how to identify the best of all permitted options. It is precisely these choices with which an ethics of virtue is primarily concerned. The great difficulty in the moral life is not in learning that acts of lying, stealing, adultery, and murder are opposed to virtue, or in resisting temptation to commit moral atrocities. Occasionally, we encounter quandary situations in which the requirements of virtue are not immediately clear, or in which we are uncertain if a particular act should be characterized as theft, for example, but they make up only a fraction of the moral life. For most of us, the greater part of the moral life has to do with such concerns as how we occupy our time, how we earn a living, how we spend our money, how we respond to adversity, how we indulge our desires, whom we associate with, and how we treat our families and neighbors. An ethics of virtue certainly has the resources for analyzing difficult situations and possesses the vocabulary for making fine but crucial distinctions between prohibited, permitted, and required acts. To a much greater degree than natural law, however, and more reliably than existential ethics, it accounts for the endeavor of living a life characterized by a settled disposition to pursue the good appropriate to each individual in the particular circumstances of his or her life alone and with others.

An ethics of virtue does this more reliably than Rahner's existential ethics because it does not rely on his problematic philosophical and anthropological presuppositions. Rahner quite rightly criticizes the traditional view of human essence, upon which the precepts of natural law are founded, as not being an eternally valid description but rather the reflection of a particular cultural view of what it is to be human. But he then substitutes a redescription in which he makes a sharp distinction between a sphere of subjective freedom and transcendence, knowable by the process of "transcendental reflection" (self-reflective meditation on the conditions for being human), and an empirically observable sphere of materiality. In other words, Rahner does not deny that there is a human essence upon which moral precepts can be based, he just denies the accuracy of previous descriptions and then claims that he has found a method for providing an adequate description.

Although I criticize Rahner's philosophical claims, I do not deny that an ethics of virtue makes controversial claims of its own—for example, that character should be the central concern of ethics, that there is an intimate connection between what we think, say, and do and who we are as moral agents, and that there can be identifiable central human goods toward which the virtues aim and in which they participate—but I do deny that an advocate of the virtues has to defend a metaphysics in the way that Rahner does. An ethics of virtue may be contingently associated with a theory of the ultimate nature of human essence and experience, but its central claims do not depend on such a theory in the way that Rahner's claims do. One can accept much of Thomas's teaching about the cardinal virtues, for example, without sharing his beliefs about God, the end for which God created the world, or Thomas's vision of ultimate human beatitude.

In his acknowledgement of Thomas as an inspiration for his moral theory, Rahner readily admits the contemporary philosophical concerns informing his study of Thomas. It is one thing to abandon the pretense of neutrality in one's approach to a historical text, however, and quite another to attribute contemporary philosophical concerns to the long-deceased author of the text one is considering. The latter project, in fact, often requires that one regard such concerns as eternal rather than merely contemporary.

One of the main differences between Rahner's appropriation of Thomas for existential ethics and the appropriation I suggest for reviving an ethics of virtue concerns the uses to which one can put a historical source. Rahner is interested in stepping outside history and outside the vocabulary available to Thomas in order to reach "the really philosophical in Thomas" (1968: xlix–1). To the extent that Rahner wants to claim Thomas for existential ethics, which presumes a modern view of the human subject and a set of philosophical concerns stemming from Kant and Heidegger, Rahner has to defend an interpretation of Thomas that presumes the ability to discern his interest in issues that Thomas lacked a vocabulary to articulate. Such a view not only presumes that moral and philosophical issues have a life that transcends the constraints of history, culture, and language, so that Aristotle, Thomas, Kant, and Rahner participate, implicitly if not explicitly, in the same timeless conversation, but it also lacks the ability to present positive textual evidence in defense of problematic interpretations. The defense has to rest on Thomas's silence on certain issues as an indication that he was not opposed to ideas attributed to him.

In contrast, the interpretation I have made of Thomas depends on the content and arrangement of the relevant texts and could be refuted by contrary textual evidence or by historical evidence that the concerns I attribute to him are anachronistic. Thomas is certainly a resource for the contemporary debate about virtue, but not because he experienced or anticipated our culture's inability to sustain a common moral vocabulary sufficient to provide participants in moral argument with mutually acceptable or even intelligible accounts of moral judgments. He is a useful resource for those who think that the vocabulary of the virtues is a promising alternative to contemporary ways of talking about ethics because in the absence of contemporary examples we can relearn that vocabulary by attending to his use of it. He does not address the problems that prompt us to look for alternative ways of conceiving the moral life and analyzing moral choices, but he provides a vocabulary that avoids those problems. One of Rahner's great insights into Thomas's moral teaching is that the problems which led to the abandonment of natural-law thinking should not be attributed to Thomas, and that his thinking about ethics tends in a different direction from empirically observable attributes of human essence upon which the natural moral law supposedly can be based. The advantage of my reading of Thomas over Rahner's is that there is more in the text to support it, and that it avoids the necessity of having to defend a problematic hermeneutics and revised view of human essence even less likely to elicit agreement than the deficient natural-law original.

The prudential ethics of virtue that I describe and attribute to Thomas also avoids some less theoretical and more practical internal problems encountered by Rahner's proposal. Despite Rahner's claims to the contrary, there is the potential for verdicts of existential ethics to conflict with verdicts of natural law. Although Rahner insists that the prohibitions of natural law can never be contravened by an existential ethical imperative, he has so drastically redescribed human essence that the traditional prohibitions have suspect foundations, and he has so privatized existential ethics that its commands are immune to challenge. There is no apparent way to adjudicate debates over the authenticity of natural-law verdicts, since the "core" of human essence is not empirically observable but only knowable by transcendental reflection. But neither is there any way to deny purported existential imperatives except by measuring them against the now-questionable negative verdicts of natural law.

In an ethics of virtue, in contrast, an agent's judgment that a particular act does or does not accord with prudence, justice, temperance, and fortitude is always open to public challenge because the only source of knowledge of what constitutes and coheres with those virtues is "public property": a community's moral experience reflected, among other ways, in its literature, its distribution of honors and punishment, its choice of heroes, and its recognition of moral authority. One has to defend one's moral point of view and judgments in terms of a community's standard of virtue. The community can be wrong, and our culture knows of instances in which critics were able to persuade a community of its corruption — the Hebrew prophets, for example, or in our own time, Martin Luther King — but in order to make their case the critics have to appeal to publicly available criteria of judgment. The vocabulary of the virtues, in other words, has its reference in a community's common experience, whereas the vocabulary of Rahner's proposed existential ethics has its reference in an individual's private experience. The knowledge that existential ethics presumes is "non-discursive" and "objectless," communicated by means of an internally experienced "pointing gesture" rather than by words.

As we have seen, Thomas unfortunately suffers the fate of being identified too closely with the tradition he inspired, with the result that many critics of the natural-law tradition think they are refuting St. Thomas in the course of dismissing a particular articulation of natural law. Or, as in Rahner's case, sympathetic attempts to correct the excesses or limitation of the tradition have little continuity with Thomas's own teaching. If Thomas is read as describing a basically Aristotelian ethics of virtue in which prudence is assigned much of the deliberative work and commanding of action that later theorists attribute to the syllogistic reasoning of natural law, Rahner's refinements are superfluous at best. If prudence does not merely apply universals to "cases," and if it can determine obligation and specify the right thing for an individual to do in a concrete and contingent situation, there is no need to appeal to anything like existential ethics as a corrective or necessary addition to prudence— unless one has independent reasons for retaining the bulk of Rahner's transcendental anthropology.

In an authentically Thomistic ethics — to sum up what has been argued in previous chapters — rather than deducing conclusions from an array of naturally known principles, one is habituated to the correct judgment of what is to be done. Prudence is the perfected or developed habit concerned with acting in accord with right reason. As Thomas says of prudence in his *Commentary on the Nicomachean Ethics,* it is the virtue "dealing with action and concerned with things good and bad for man," both in matters of justice in social relations and in the development of an individual's own character (*Commentary* 1177, 1259). Unlike the certain conclusions of the speculative sciences, the conclusions of prudence, which deals with practical matters, the "contingent individual incidents, which form the setting for human acts," are only probable (*S.T.* II-II, q. 47, a. 9). Prudence deals with the singular as opposed to the universal (*Commentary* 1247). Its judgments are conjectural and deliberative (*Commentary* 1174 and 1189), the opposite of nondiscursive, involving a determination of "what happens in the majority of cases" (*S.T.* II-II, q. 47, a. 3). Prudence is related to universals in that it possesses knowledge of "general moral principles of reason," but its main focus is on the "individual situations in which human actions take place" (ibid.). Thomas goes so far as to say that if it were necessary for an individual to have only one kind of knowledge, one ought to choose knowledge of "particulars" because as this kind of knowledge is "closer to operation" it is more likely to lead to right action (*Commentary* 1194).

The development or perfection of prudence depends, in large part, on memory, maturity, and education. It uses principles that "are not inherited with human nature, but are discovered through experience and instruction" (*S.T.* II-II, q. 47, a. 15). One becomes prudent through practice (a. 16) and through the "seasoning" of time (a. 3), so that one is gradually and progressively enabled to deal with situations and to make a decision in the way a wise individual "would so decide it" (a. 7). Rather than looking to universal rules for guidance about a future course of action, prudence "learns from the past and present" (a. 1).

Right reason about things to be done, or about "means," according to Thomas, also requires that one be correctly oriented to ends, which depends on the rightness of one's appetites or inclinations, the dominion of the other cardinal moral virtues. (*S.T.* I-II, q. 57, a. 4). Thomas was engaged in reconciling an Aristotelian ethic of habituated virtues with a Christianized Stoic ethic of law in which the divinely promulgated natural law is part of the makeup of human minds. To be sure, Thomas modifies the Aristotelian virtue ethic, but nonetheless the epistemic significance of the element of law in his synthesis is subordinated to the element of virtue. The role of law is theological and explanatory: Whereas Aristotle sees human orientation to political goods, Thomas insists on the Augustinian notion of human orientation to God as the final end. This Christian understanding of human ends changes the role played by prudence in that Thomas views the first principles of natural law, knowable by synderesis, as the first principles of practical reason. They function as a divinely created framework within which prudence operates, as a theological explanation for agreement about its judgments, and as an account of how we are motivated to act at all. For Aristotle, in contrast, prudence or phronesis operates without first principles.

Thomas's first principles, however, play a relatively restricted role. The naturally known first principle of practical reason—that good is to be pursued and evil avoided—functions much like the so-called law of noncontradiction, the first principle in Thomas's account of the speculative sciences, stating that nothing can both be and not be at the same time. That we pursue what we perceive as good and avoid what we regard as evil is not the sort of principle from which specific conclusions can be drawn. It applies to all of our practical reasoning, not just to our reasoning about right and wrong.

In most cases, determinations of practical as well as speculative principles that actually are used for guiding thinking or behavior are made on the basis of what appears to happen most of the time. The first principles of natural law are associated, of course, with Thomas's list of natural inclinations. Although stated as rules on occasion, they primarily have to do with the achievement of goods. As rules or general principles, they are so abstract and general that they are devoid of any meaning except that which they receive in conjunction with the operation of the cardinal virtues under the direction of prudence. Prudence, rather than synderesis, determines what it actually means to act according to right reason in each case. This is where Thomas joins natural law and Aristotelian virtue. He associates the principle or inclination to preserve "being" with the virtue of fortitude, the inclination to achieve the goods necessary for the sustenance of life with temperance, and the inclinations to live in society and to know God with justice and prudence.

Synderesis, which perceives first principles, only determines the most general ends of any human action, which is always aimed at obtaining some good; prudence acting in accord with right appetite and directing or perfecting the operation of the virtues determines the means of obtaining the good, what actions in particular are to be done (*S.T.* II-II, q. 47, a. 6). Prudence, not a syllogistic application of the formal principles of the natural law that express those ends generally, determines and commands what is to be done in order to achieve those ends on the basis of counsel and judgment (I-II, q. 57, a. 6.; cf. II-II, q. 47, aa. 8–9) and in light of its experienced understanding of the common good (II-II, q. 47, a. 10).

Natural law plays no significant epistemic function in making practical moral determinations. It functions formally to account for the judgments of prudence. In order to carry out the actual work of determining what is to be done, prudence needs much more than the general precepts of natural law and an understanding of the circumstance in question. Prudence both shapes and is shaped by the virtues and general social agreement about the goods to which they are oriented. That is, rather than relying on the intuitions of synderesis and applying them syllogistically to circumstances, prudence depends on education into the customary judgments of society about what human goods in particular are appropriate and about how they are to be achieved. The judgments of prudence, in turn, become part of the content of moral education, which informs moral deliberation. Thomas notes that prudence has to do with things about which we deliberate, and that to deliberate well about what is to be done is the sign of a prudent individual (*Commentary* 1189). He summarizes the mutual dependence of prudence and the virtues by observing, for example, that "the happiness of active living, which is gauged by the activities of the moral virtues, is attributed to prudence perfecting all the moral virtues" (2111).

Making moral determinations, for Thomas, is not a matter of applying universal laws to situations. Prudence attends to singulars, both to singular individuals and to unique circumstances. It does not regard an individual as only an instance of humanity in general, but then again it does not grant moral authority to each individual's autonomous subjective awareness, and it regards situations as contingent rather than as "cases." It does not limit freedom by confining obligation to a rigid and content-laden articulation of the natural law, but then again it does not make the achievement of a particular conception of freedom a moral imperative. Prudence is especially concerned with specifying what particular choice out of all the permitted possibilities is to be made here and now by an individual or a community. That specification and its consequent command is made by reference to the common good and within the context of agreement about virtues and ends.

IV

So far, I have been stressing the implications of my reading of Thomas for distinctively Roman Catholic ethics, but those implications extend to Christian ethics in general and to philosophical ethics as well. An especially far-reaching implication, I believe, is that Thomas provides a vocabulary for moral discourse in which Christians and non-Christians can participate equally. As I noted in Chapter 3, a full account of Thomas's ethics would attend to the theological virtues and especially to charity and would describe their relation to the cardinal moral virtues that I have described. I also noted, however, that Thomas abstracts to a certain degree from his theological framework and talks in great detail about the virtue and happiness attainable in this life by Christians as well as "pagans."

This is not at all to say that a theory of the virtues somehow compels assent by Christians and agreement by others. The claim is only that accounts of the moral life similar to Thomas's are available to non-Christians because there is no requirement that anyone using this vocabulary of the virtues also use, or even understand, a theological vocabulary. Moreover, even if an ethics of prudential virtue fails to inspire assent by non-Christians, it remains the case that it is something about which Christians and non-Christians can converse on an equal footing. Although Thomas's articulation of this ethics has a profound theological context, it is not theology upon which its coherence hinges. Thomas's main source for the cardinal virtues is Aristotle, and although there is considerable room for debate about the thoroughness of Aristotle's baptism by Thomas, the fact remains that most of Thomas's teaching about virtue is an account of morality with which nonbaptized Aristotelians can agree. In short, the factors precluding agreement with or understanding of the Thomistic account of prudential virtue have little to do with religion but a great deal to do with the contemporary ways in which both religious and nonreligious discourse about ethics is conducted. Modern Christians and Jews are just as likely to be puzzled or affronted by this account as modern pagans.

Despite the equality of access to a conversation about this ethics, Christians convinced of the desirability of using its vocabulary need not dilute their theological claims or their distinctively Christian moral points of view. This is not a reduction of moral claims to the lowest possible common denominator of all rational agents for the sake of agreement on principles of justice, as is arguably the case in John Rawls's theory (Rawls 1971; see Jeffrey Stout's discussion of this criticism of Rawls in 1981: 218-43. See also Harlan R. Beckley's response to Stout and affirmation of the usefulness of Rawls for discourse between Christians and non-Christians in 1985: 210-42, especially 222-25). By saying this, I am not making claims about the distinctiveness of Christian ethics, a related but separable concern, but rather calling attention to a contemporary implication of Thomas's claim that there is a level of virtue and a kind of corresponding happiness that is not the exclusive property of Christians. From Thomas's Christian perspective, however, the discussion and exercise of the cardinal virtues of prudence, temperance, justice, and fortitude do not exhaust the topic of the Christian moral life. As Stanley Hauerwas points out,

> [F]or Aquinas there is a good that sustains and orders all the relative goods of our existence. The moral correlative of this metaphysical claim is that for any virtue to be true virtue it must be ordered by charity—i.e., it must be directed to God [*S.T.* II-II, q. 23, a. 7]. Thomas does not deny that an act or virtue can lack charity and still be good in the sense that it fulfills its particular object. But such virtue is not good in the full sense, because it does not contribute to the unity of the self that is possible only when the self is directed to its true end. In other words virtues or

> actions that lack charity are not less good in effects than those
> formed by charity, but what is at stake is not the act or virtue in
> itself, but the agent. It is the kind of agent that the act or virtue
> lacking charity forms that makes it less than true. (1975: 81–82)

Hauerwas adds in a footnote the useful reminder that "Aquinas is not writing to recommend the kind of moral life possible without charity, though such a life is possible and important, but rather to commend the life that should be characteristic of Christians who have been graced with charity" (1975: 82). This is all to say that Christians and non-Christians can agree about the shape of the moral life characterized by prudential virtue and continue to disagree about the extent to which prudence encompasses the whole of the moral life. This is a highly desirable situation for moral discourse, allowing us to retain the relevance of the metaphor of conversation. It not only preserves for Christians the integrity of their self-understanding while simultaneously permitting a level of moral agreement sufficient to keep the peace in a pluralistic society, but it also permits each party in the encounter between religious and nonreligious thinking to question and be questioned by the other. The Thomistic account of prudential virtue thus has implications for more than specifically Christian ethics. It has implications for practical ethics and for moral theory whether or not our thinking about these matters is theologically informed. (For relevant discussions of the relationship between religion and morality, as well as the relationship between notions of virtue and notions of obligation, see Frederick S. Carney, 1973, and Hauerwas, 1975.) Other participants in contemporary discussion of virtue theory, most notably Pieper (1965), Hauerwas (1974, 1975, 1981), MacIntyre (1981), William M. Sullivan (1982), and Meilaender (1984), have already said a great deal in the way of description of various understandings of virtue ethics and in defense of the vocabulary of the virtues as an alternative to most of modern moral philosophy. Corrections and additions to those accounts are certainly in order, but rather than trying to make them here I want to conclude by calling attention to some of the implications of the foregoing study of prudence in particular for practicing the moral life and for reflecting upon it.

A plausible although not uncontestable way of identifying an ethics of virtue, as contrasted with other accounts of morality, is by asking whether there is a concern for particular virtues. If one thinks that moral discourse and practice would be better off if we were once again to employ a vocabulary that referred to particular virtues, then we need to rehabilitate the vocabulary by actually using the relevant words and grammar. For the sake of clarity, for consistency between theory and practice, and for strategic reasons, we should describe agents and their acts as prudent, temperate, courageous, and just (and in terms of the opposite vices, as the case may be), or in terms of whatever other habitual traits of character one wishes to promote as virtues. (Not much rides on whether we retain Thomas's list of the four cardinal virtues, although I see no pressing reason to modify it.) There are different difficulties associated with reclaiming each of the cardinal virtues, which suffer from a modern contraction of their classical meanings. Temperance has primarily come to mean restraint in the consumption of food and drink; the appropriateness of fearing real dangers has dropped out of our understanding of courage, which some see as a vice in the nuclear age; justice has lost its connection to persons and is regarded almost exclusively as an attribute of legal systems and social structures; and prudence has become mere carefulness or even excessive concern for self-interest.

For the most part, however, we still favor the traits of character included in the classical understanding of the virtues, whether or not we give those traits their classical labels. It still is intelligible to praise people who show reasonable restraint and order in the satisfaction of their desires, who take sensible stands against adversity, who demand for themselves no more than what is due and grant to others what they deserve, and who respond appropriately to a realistic assessment of the circumstances of life. One of the implicit suggestions of this study has been that in order to reestablish a continuity between our contemporary moral discourse and a largely supplanted way of talking that described people characterized by these dispositions as temperate, brave, just, and prudent, we need to investigate what someone like Thomas meant when he talked about individual virtues, which is what I have tried to do in the case of prudence. Then we need to experiment with the vocabulary ourselves, for example in the way that Gilbert Meilaender does when he talks about the vice of curiosity and the virtue of gratitude (1984: 127–75).

The vocabulary may need refinement. In many cases it may be inadequate as a description of dispositions desirable in our situation. The issue, however, is not whether we use the same words to talk about character but the role that character has in our understanding of the moral life. Stanley Hauerwas's characterization of the situation-ethics debate as "parochial" can be applied to other debates current in contemporary ethics: "All sides assume that the primary issue for moral behavior is the decision we make about particular situations and practices. As a result, it is forgotten that what is at stake is not the act itself, but the kind of person we will be" (1975: 7). The judgment about the relative importance of character is itself controversial, of course, but less controversial is the potential for enrichment of our moral discourse if we attended to it more carefully. "To stress the importance of the idea of character," Hauerwas points out, " . . . is an attempt to broaden the phenomenology of moral experience beyond that assumed by those who think judgments are the only aspect of moral experience open to rational reflection" (1975: 29). He correctly observes that at least for Thomas Aquinas, this concern for character is the focus of prudence:

> The condition that is necessary for each virtue to be absolute is that it be formed through prudence (moral wisdom), for it is prudence alone that not only confers the aptness for good work but also its use. Therefore, all the other moral virtues are dependent upon and find their unity in the operation of prudence. It does not seem to be an unwarranted conclusion that this unity given to the virtues by prudence at least seems to have some similarities to what we mean by character, for the good of prudence is the good of the agent himself. (1975: 79)

Fortunately, there still is some continuity between our present vocabulary and the tradition of virtue. Our culture obviously contains communities of people who share common backgrounds, interests, activities, beliefs, and practices: civic organizations, religious communities, educational institutions, the military services, and athletic teams, to name a few. What is significant about such groups is that they have a sufficient sense of common purpose to recognize and approve traits of character that not only further those purposes but which when exercised are seen as good in themselves. (See Sullivan, 1982, and Bellah et al., 1985, for a discussion of this theme and identification of communities concerned with character. For a discussion of the erosion of the virtues in the Christian community, as well as an attempt to identify resources for their recovery, see Turner, 1985.)

An important political implication of this study is that the vestiges of the tradition of the virtues in our national community need to be preserved and fostered by recognizing and encouraging the communities that practice it. This is not to say that all of the habitual traits of character esteemed by associations of people with shared interests are worthy of cultivation by the rest of us: The goods to which those dispositions are oriented might be far from goods that are truly common. I am suggesting, however, that certain communities have a way of thinking about the relation between character and behavior that makes an ethics of virtue intelligible, and that the habits practiced in some existing communities are genuinely moral virtues. The honest acknowledgment of sources, a trait valued by the academic community, for example, is a form of justice. Some of these communities may be corrupt: Some members of the athletic community may be perverting their common good through the sale and use of narcotics, or segments of the military community may be guilty of illicit violence. What makes such instances of intemperance and injustice recognizable as the vices they are, however, is agreement on a set of shared goods threatened by vice and an understanding of character and behavior that values the opposing virtues.

There is no knowledge of virtues and vices outside of a community whose purposes and conception of the good creates them. Individuals do not learn the virtues in isolation. While individuals may learn from stories that recount the exercise of various virtues, illustrate their meaning, and inspire their pursuit, practical knowledge of the virtues, unlike theoretical knowledge, cannot be obtained from textbooks. Even the narratives about virtue are dependent on the practice of communities that produce and preserve them. A dissertation about prudence has little to do with the actual development of prudence in its author or readers in the absence of a context in which the virtues are demonstrated by the practically wise and emulated by the inexperienced.

In short, if we want to recover and preserve the vocabulary of virtue, we need to employ it, and we cannot employ it intelligibly in the absence of a context that sustains it. In this respect, the resuscitation of the language of virtue is analogous to attempts to revive any expiring language. There is something futile about struggling to preserve Yiddish, Creole, or Native American languages unless there is a simultaneous struggle to preserve the communities that use them. When we do employ the virtues in our vocabulary, we need to focus our moral discourse and concern on character instead of almost exclusively on acts. And when we do analyze the morality of acts, we would do well to employ something like Thomas's construal of the circumstances of acts in order to maintain a concern for the moral condition of the agent performing the act.

I began this study by saying that I intended it both as a contribution and as a challenge to contemporary discussion of an ethics of virtue. If I have been successful, the contribution consists in making progress toward the rehabilitation of Thomas Aquinas as a resource for understanding a significant way of thinking about morality in terms of the virtues. In particular, I have tried to make some progress toward the rehabilitation of the specific virtue of prudence. If we follow Thomas in understanding prudence as the perfection of practical reason, we will be well on the way toward reclaiming an ethics of virtue.

The challenge I hope I have made is to have suggested the need for a considerable amount of additional historical work, moral practice, and political activity. There is a need for continued reexamination of the received history of moral thought, for refinement of the existing revisionist histories (for a good example, see Richard J. Mouw's 1985 critique of Alasdair MacIntyre's reading of Reformation ethics), for narrations of the virtue tradition or traditions in particular, and for a reappraisal of figures who might be Thomas's successors. Perhaps our presumption that Thomas was teaching a doctrine of natural law has led us similarly to misread those who drew on Thomas and to neglect the potential connections between Thomas and those who talked about the virtues instead of natural law.

Beyond that kind of historical study, with the exception of Gilbert Meilaender's recent work (1984) and Josef Pieper's treatment of the cardinal virtues (1965), we have little in the way of contemporary explication of individual virtues. Most of the academic conversation concerned with the virtues tends to be about the vocabulary of virtue without actually employing it. We are likewise lacking examples of the application of an ethics of virtue to concrete moral problems. (Hauerwas's discussion of caring for the mentally disabled, 1985, is a notable exception.) This deficiency may reflect a reluctance by those interested in the virtues to return to modern moral philosophy's preoccupation with "quandary ethics," to the extent that it is concerned with practical moral problems at all. There is nonetheless a need for reflection on the kinds of action that would be characteristic of a person with virtuous dispositions when such a person is confronted with the most difficult of concrete moral choices, however rarely one might actually encounter them. We need to articulate what is the prudent, temperate, brave, and just thing to do in situations where, for example, the taking or preservation of human life is at stake. The dominant strains of modern moral philosophy have highly sophisticated, although vulnerable, proposals for making such moral choices. So far, those concerned with the virtues have presented few alternatives.

Finally, I hope I have suggested the need for what amounts to a political concern for the ways in which the kinds of communities and activities that sustain the practice of virtue can be cultivated. Unless those communities can flourish, unless virtuous activities can attract the interest and participation of the larger community, the vocabulary of the virtues will continue to be misunderstood and neglected, and our common moral discourse will continue to be dominated by unsatisfactory alternatives.

My vision of the future of our moral discourse is not as dark as Alasdair MacIntyre's: Some communities in which the vocabulary of virtue has currency still exist or even flourish, the virtues may not be as foreign to our everyday moral conversation as they are to philosophical discussion, the philosophical liberalism undergirding many of our political institutions and practices has at least succeeded in preserving space and toleration for more traditional ways of conceiving moral and political life, and conversation among those of us who disagree continues to be a possible alternative to violence. Because the virtues are still being practiced, probably by most of us to some extent, I doubt that the "new dark ages" are immediately at hand (MacIntyre 1981: 245). We still have sufficient experience in the virtues to understand, although perhaps with difficulty, someone like Thomas. We still value prudential reasoning, even if we are suspicious of its legitimate title. And the dominant intellectual and moral traditions may have more continuity with more traditional modes of practical reasoning than their critics suppose.

Nonetheless, a consideration that I have already alluded to makes my practical political concerns pressing. That consideration was summed up for me by a teacher who described it as the "winner-take-all" understanding of history: The security of our history, in this case our moral heritage, is never guaranteed. History consists in the stories we tell ourselves and our children about the past, stories which vary depending on the identity and perspective of the narrator. Some of them more faithfully recount the experience and self-understanding of various communities than others, and none of the stories exists apart from the telling of them. When we find it difficult to hear or understand the voices expressing the moral experience or understanding of communities that cultivated the virtues, we are in danger of losing them permanently, because the virtues are not abstract principles expressed in the timeless voice of reason but rather products of a community's practice. There is no way of knowing if the present partial eclipse of the virtues is reversing, whether a recent revival of philosophical interest is an aberration, or whether they will be obscured entirely. But even if the coming age is dim rather than dark, a total eclipse of the virtues would be permanent, and we would have to look for illumination somewhere else. The existing alternatives are not very promising, and that gives a concern for the cultivation of virtue its urgency.

Sources

Aquinas, St. Thomas
   1947   *Summa Theologica.* 3 vols. Fathers of the English Dominican Province, trans. New York: Benziger Brothers.
   1951   *Treatise on the Virtues (In General).* John Patrick Reid, trans. Providence, R.I.: The Providence College Press.
   1952   *Summa Theologiae.* Latin edition. Rome: Marietti Editori.
   1952   *The Disputed Questions on Truth.* Robert Mulligan, trans. Chicago: Henry Regnery.
   1963   *Treatise on Happiness* [*S.T.* I–II, qq. 1–21]. John A. Oesterle, trans. Englewood Cliffs, N.J.: Prentice-Hall (rpt. 1983, University of Notre Dame Press).
   1964   *Commentary on the Nicomachean Ethics.* C. I. Litzinger, trans. Chicago: Henry Regnery.
   1964   *Summa Theologiae.* Blackfriars English and Latin edition. New York: McGraw-Hill.
   1966   *Treatise on the Virtues* [*S.T.* I–II, qq. 49–67]. John A. Oesterle, trans. Englewood Cliffs, N.J.: Prentice-Hall.
Aristotle
   1946   *The Politics of Aristotle.* Ernest Barker, trans. Oxford: Clarendon Press (rpt. 1981, Oxford University Press).
   1953   *The Ethics of Aristotle: The Nicomachean Ethics.* J.A.K. Thomson, trans. Revised translation by Hugh Tredennick, 1976. London: Penguin Classics.
Armstrong, R. A.
   1966   *Primary and Secondary Precepts in Thomistic Natural Law Teaching.* The Hague: Martinus Nijhoff.

Beckley, Harlan R.
    1985   "A Christian Affirmation of Rawls' Idea of Justice as Fairness — Part I." In
           Journal of Religious Ethics 13, no. 2 (Fall): 210-42.
Bellah, Robert, Richard Madson, William M. Sullivan, Ann Swidler, Steven M. Tipton
    1985   *Habits of the Heart.* Berkeley and Los Angeles: University of California Press.
Bresnahan, James F.
    1970   "Rahner's Christian Ethics." In *America* 123 (October): 351-54.
    1972   "The Methodology of 'Natural Law' Ethical Reasoning in the Theology
           of Karl Rahner, and its Supplementary Development Using the Legal
           Philosophy of Lon L. Fuller." Ph.D. dissertation, Yale University.
    1976   "Rahner's Ethics: Critical Natural Law in Relation to Contemporary
           Ethical Methodology." In *Journal of Religion* 56 (January): 36-60.
Brown, B. F.
    1967   "Natural Law." In the Catholic University of America's *New Catholic
           Encyclopedia*, vol. 10 (1967). New York: McGraw Hill. 251-56.
Carney, Frederick S.
    1973   "The Virtue-Obligation Controversy." In *Journal of Religious Ethics* 1,
           no. 1: 5-19.
Cicero, Marcus Tullius
    1907   *On the Nature of the Gods: On Divination, On Fate, On the Republic, On
           the Laws, and On Standing for the Counsulship.* C. D. Yonge, trans.
           London: George Bell.
    1929   *On the Common Wealth.* George Holland Sabine and Stanley Barney
           Smith, trans. Columbus: Ohio State University Press.
Clarke, Samuel
    1732   *A Discourse Concerning the Being and Attributes of God, the Obliga-
           tions of Natural Religion, and the Truth and Certainty of the Christian
           Revelation . . .* London: J&J Knaplon.
Copleston, F. C., S.J.
    1955   *Aquinas.* London: Penguin Books.
D'Arcy, Eric
    1961   *Conscience and Its Right to Freedom.* New York: Sheed and Ward.
Defarrari, Roy J.
    1960   *A Latin-English Dictionary of St. Thomas Aquinas.* Boston: Daughters
           of St. Paul.
Engberg-Pedersen, Troels
    1983   *Aristotle's Theory of Moral Insight.* New York: Clarendon Press.
Dorr, Donal J.
    1969   "Karl Rahner's Formal Existential Ethics." In *Irish Theological Quarterly*
           36 (July): 211-29.
d'Entreves, A. P.
    1951   *Natural Law: An Introduction to Legal Philosophy.* London: Hutchinson's
           University Library.
Finnis, John
    1980   *Natural Law and Natural Rights.* Oxford: Clarendon Press.

Fletcher, Joseph
 1966 *Situation Ethics.* (Paperback edition 1974, Philadelphia: Westminster Press).
Gilleman, Gerard, S.J.
 1959 *The Primacy of Charity in Moral Theology.* William F. Ryan, S.J., and Andre Vachon, S.J., trans. Westminster, Md.: The Newman Press.
Gustafson, James
 1968 *Christ and the Moral Life.* New York: Harper & Row.
Hartmann, Herbert E., Jr.
 1979 "St. Thomas and Prudence." Ph.D. dissertation, University of Toronto.
Hauerwas, Stanley
 1974 *Vision and Virtue.* Notre Dame, Ind.: Fides/Claretian.
 1975 *Character and the Christian Life.* San Antonio, Tex.: Trinity University Press.
 1975 "Obligation and Virtue Once More." In *Journal of Religious Ethics* 3, no. 1 (Spring):27–44.
 1981 *A Community of Character.* Notre Dame, Ind.: University of Notre Dame Press.
 1986 *Suffering Presence: Theological Reflections on Medicine, the Mentally Handicapped, and the Church.* Notre Dame, Ind.: University of Notre Dame Press.
Higgins, Thomas J.
 1958 *Man as Man: The Science and Art of Ethics.* Revised edition. Milwaukee, Wisc.: Bruce Publishing.
Hobbes, Thomas
 1958 *Leviathan.* New York: Macmillan.
Hume, David
 1896 *A Treatise of Human Nature.* Oxford: Clarendon Press.
Jaffa, Harry V.
 1952 *Thomism and Aristotelianism; A Study of the Commentary by Thomas Aquinas on the Nicomachean Ethics.* Chicago: University of Chicago Press.
Joachim, Harold Henry
 1951 Aristotle. *The Nicomachean Ethics; A Commentary.* D. A. Rees, ed. Oxford: Clarendon Press.
Kant, Immanuel
 1976 *Groundwork of the Metaphysics of Morals.* H. J. Paten, trans. London: Hutchinson University Library.
Levy, Sanford S.
 1985 "Richard McCormick and Proportionate Reason." In *Journal of Religious Ethics* 13, no. 2 (Fall):258–72.
Locke, John
 1952 *Two Treatises of Government.* Thomas P. Peardon, ed. New York: Liberal Arts Press.

Lottin, Odon
    1931   *Le Droit Natural Chez s. Thomas et ses Predecessures.* Bruges.
McCormick, Richard, and Ramsey, Paul, eds.
    1978   *Doing Evil to Achieve Good.* Chicago: Loyola University Press.
MacIntyre, Alasdair
    1971   *Against the Self-Images of the Age.* Notre Dame, Ind.: University of Notre
           Dame Press (paperback ed. 1978).
    1981   *After Virtue: A Study In Moral Theory.* Notre Dame, Ind.: University of
           Notre Dame Press.
Meilaender, Gilbert
    1984   *The Theory and Practice of Virtue.* Notre Dame, Ind.: University of Notre
           Dame Press.
Mouw, Richard J.
    1985   "Alasdair MacIntyre on Reformation Ethics." In *Journal of Religious Ethics*
           13, no. 2 (Fall):243–57.
Nelson, Daniel M.
    1987   "Karl Rahner's Existential Ethics." In *The Thomist* 51, no. 3 (July):461–79.
O'Connor, D. J.
    1967   *Aquinas and Natural Law.* London: Macmillan.
Pieper, Josef
    1965   *The Four Cardinal Virtues.* New York: Harcourt Brace Jovanovich (paper-
           back ed. 1966, Notre Dame, Ind.: University of Notre Dame Press).
Plato
    1968   *The Republic.* Allan Bloom, trans. New York: Basic Books.
Preller, Victor
    1967   *Divine Science and the Science of God: A Reformulation of Thomas
           Aquinas.* Princeton, N.J.: Princeton University Press.
Pufendorf, Samuel, freiherr von
    1703   *On the Law of Nature and Nations.* Oxford: L. Litchfield.
Quay, Paul M., S.J.
    1985   "The Disvalue of Ontic Evil." In *Theological Studies* 46, (June):263–86.
Rahner, Karl
    1950   "Gefahren im heutigen Katholizismus." Einsiedeln: Bensizer. The essay
           appears in English as "Dangers in Catholicism Today," in *Nature and
           Grace,* trans. Dinah Wharton. New York: Sheed and Ward, 1964.
    1961   "Concerning the Relationship between Nature and Grace." In *Theologi-
           cal Investigations,* vol. 1. Cornelius Ernst, trans. Baltimore: Helicon
           Press.
    1963   "On the Question of a Formal Existential Ethics." In *Theological Investiga-
           tions,* vol. 2. Karl-H. Kruger, trans. Baltimore: Helicon Press.
    1963   "The Dignity and Freedom of Man." In *Theological Investigations,* vol. 2.
           Karl-H. Kruger, trans. Baltimore: Helicon Press.
    1964   *The Dynamic Element in the Church.* W. J. O'Hara, trans. New York:
           Herder and Herder.
    1968   *Spirit in the World.* William Dych, trans. New York: Herder and Herder.

1969   "Theology of Freedom." In *Theological Investigations,* vol. 4. Karl-H.
        and Boniface Kruger, trans. Baltimore: Helicon Press.
1972   "The Problem of Genetic Manipulation." In *Theological Investigations,*
        vol. 9. Graham Harrison, trans. London: Darton, Longman & Todd.
1972   "The Experiment With Man." In *Theological Investigations,* vol. 9. Gra-
        ham Harrison, trans. London: Darton, Longman & Todd.

Rawls, John
1971   *A Theory of Justice.* Cambridge, Mass.: Belknap Press.
Rommen, Heinrich
1936   Die Ewige Weiderkehr des Naturrechts. T. R. Hanley, trans., 1947, as *The
        Natural Law.* St. Louis: B. Berder Book Co.
Sabine, George
1937   *A History of Political Theory.* New York: Henry Holt.
Sigmund, Paul
1971   *Natural Law in Political Thought.* Cambridge, Mass.: Winthrop Publishers.
Sophocles
1954   *Antigone.* Elizabeth Wycoff, trans. In *The Complete Greek Tragedies,*
        vol. 2 (1959). David Green and Richmond Lattimore, eds. Chicago: Uni-
        versity of Chicago Press.
Spinnenweber, Andrew E.
1972   "Practical Knowledge in the Thought of St. Thomas Aquinas." Doctoral
        dissertation. Duquesne University.
Stout, Jeffrey
1981   *The Flight from Authority: Religion, Morality, and the Quest for Autonomy.*
        Notre Dame, Ind.: University of Notre Dame Press.
1985   "Virtue, Velleity, and the Ethics of War: Uses and Abuses of Aquinas'
        Ethics." Unpublished.
Strauss, Leo
1968   "Natural Law." In *International Encyclopedia of the Social Sciences,*
        vol. 2 (1968). David L. Sills, ed. New York: Macmillan.
Sullivan, William M.
1982   *Reconstructing Public Philosophy.* Berkeley and Los Angeles: University
        of California Press.
Turner, Philip
1985   *Sex, Money & Power.* Cambridge, Mass.: Crowley Publications.
Wadell, Paul J.
1985   "An Interpretation of Aquinas' Treatise on the Passions, the Virtues, and
        the Gifts from the Perspective of Charity as Friendship with God." Doctoral
        Dissertation, University of Notre Dame.
Wallace, William A.
1963   "The Existential Ethics of Karl Rahner: A Thomistic Appraisal." In the
        Thomist 27, (April-July–October): 493–515.
Wollheim, Richard
1967   "Natural Law." In *The Encyclopedia of Philosophy,* vol. 5-6 (1972). Paul
        Edwards, ed. New York: Macmillan.

INDEX